Both-And!

A Layman's Guide to Resolve the Calvinist-Arminian Divide

Both-And!

A Layman's Guide
to Resolve the
Calvinist-Arminian Divide

by

S. Maxwell

For communication write to:

both-andbook@outlook.com

*Dedicated to my Calvinist Friend
who challenged me to consider and
investigate his beliefs,
and then had the intellectual integrity
to change his position as a result of
looking at Scripture together.*

Table of Contents

Introduction 9

Part 1
The Zipper

Chapter 1: The Net Effect of a Vibrant Faith 13
Chapter 2: How to String the Cable Of Faith 17
Chapter 3: What Hampers Us in Stringing the Cables of
Faith From One Side to the Other? 25
Chapter 4: Bridging the Gap 35
Chapter 5: Putting It All Together 53

Part 2
My Personal Journey in Understanding and Evaluating Calvinism

Chapter 6: The Approach 59
Chapter 7: Calvinism's View of God's Sovereignty 61
Chapter 8: What Does the Bible Say About God's
Character? 65
Chapter 9: Can Man Make Moral Decisions, Or Not? 75
Chapter 10: Revealing Questions 81
Chapter 11: Some Passages Calvinists Use 89
Chapter 12: Romans 9 93
Chapter 13: Romans 8:29-30 99
Chapter 14: Serious Biblical Problems in this View 103
Chapter 15: A Look at the Calvinist TULIP 105
Chapter 16: Conclusion of the Issue 129

Introduction

In one sense God has carefully equipped me to write this book. A number of years ago I was challenged to consider Calvinism by a fellow who heard me speak.

My never having been taught anything about Calvinism or Arminianism was a positive aspect of our dialogue, I believe. I came to my study of these two systems without any inherited prejudice for or against either one. I can honestly say that I tried to come with an open mind to research Calvinism, looking for what Scripture had to say rather than working from any predetermined position

I worked through the arguments given me and compared them to Scripture. Then I sat down and wrote a paper to lay out what I had learned—which is the second half of this book. I include it with the hope that it might help others to think through the issues.

Along with the motive to help others think through the issues, is another, higher motive for writing this book. I want to encourage a redirection of the immense amount of time, energy, passion and money that has been spent defending "one side" and attacking the "other side." Think what would have happened if all these resources had been expended in spreading the gospel and building up the church.

The first section of this short book is a call to come together on the basis of Scripture, to see each other as brothers and sisters, not as opponents or the enemy. Let's join forces against the real enemy, Satan, uniting with the Father in what He wants to accomplish in reaching the world and edifying the church.

In Romans 15:5-6 God states this desire as a prayer we can use, "May the God who gives endurance and encouragement give [us] *the same attitude of mind toward each other that Christ Jesus had,* so that *with one mind and one voice [we] may glorify the God* and Father of our Lord Jesus Christ." That should be our goal.

As you read this, I hope that you will be able to set aside the positions that you have been taught, if they hamper you from opening yourself up to the full-orbed truth of Scripture. May God's Word be your measure, not any attempt at a systematic theology, by me or anyone else. Such theologies can be useful tools, but they must bow to Scripture, not the other way around.

May we increasingly grasp the greatness of the God we worship as revealed in His Word: perfect in love and wisdom, power and grace, complex beyond comprehension and the One who is worthy of our unfettered worship.

Part 1

The Zipper

Chapter 1
The Net Effect of a Vibrant Faith

My two sons and I were discussing the differences among various theological positions, when they came up with an illustration that I found very helpful.

It starts with a picture of the valley of the unknown: a very deep chasm with its depths shrouded in fog so, no one fully can discern all that is down there as seen in the illustration below.

On both sides of the valley are great steel eyelets representing different facets of biblical truth. These come in pairs, one on each side of the cliffs, and from a human point of view, they appear to be contradictory or paradoxical.

For instance, on one side, God is one but on the other God is three. Here's a short list of other seemingly paradoxical truths in the Word.

- While on earth Jesus was fully God and fully human.
- God hates sin, but loves sinners.
- God does not tolerate evil, yet Christ came to live in this sin-filled world.
- Jesus is absolutely holy, yet He became sin for us.
- God is just, yet He made mercy triumph over justice.
- Christians are both saints and sinners.
- Jesus is both the Lamb of God and the Lion of Judah.
- Scripture is divinely inspired but written by fallible human authors.

Over the centuries writers of theological systems have tended to pick one side of a truth and build a castle by it.[1]

Then their followers proceed to shoot arrows at those who have chosen the opposite position and have built their castle on the other side of the valley of the unknown.

Each side is utterly confident that theirs is the exclusively right understanding of Scripture and are willing to die for their position—and unfortunately, some of them have been willing to kill and persecute others for it.[2]

Each believes that they now have God figured out and so don't need any other input. They have effectually taken the tension out of their faith, eliminating what was difficult to understand and made for themselves a much more comfortable position. Their God is understandable, always predictable and tame.

The biblical position, however, is to accept both sides, realizing that what appears to be contradictory to our small minds, can be wisely and easily fit together in God's. If God has

---

[1] Jesus is God and man: Nestorians focused only on Christ's humanity; Monophisites say he was only God. God hates sin, but loves sinners: mainline theology majors on God's love, denies his wrath. Christians are both Saints and sinners: Holiness theology says we are no longer sinners. Scripture is divinely inspired but written by fallible human authors: Modern theologies deny the infallibility of Scripture.

[2] For instance: the inquisition; and believers burned at the stake in England for reading or translating Scripture, or jailed for rejecting a particular view of the Eucharist or refusing infant baptism—all as described in *Foxes' Book of Martyrs.*

put both aspects into the Bible, then we need to believe both, even if we can't figure out how they mesh.

To return to our illustration of the valley of the unknown, God asks us to believe all He says in His Word, including seemingly paradoxical statements (which He knows are compatible) and in so doing to string the cable of faith from one eyelet to the other forming a network of faith, as in the picture below.

Then God wants us to camp out on this network of faith. This is scary because we are suspended over nothing, and the net can move as we walk about. But in faith we can live there *because* of the tension of the cables, the tension of not understanding all, while believing that God does know all and we can trust Him in it.

In contrast, the theological systems created by Calvin and Arminius are meant to be a "safe" place, taking much of the tension out of faith, by staying on one side or the other, either cutting the cables of faith, or refusing to string them. This would be comparable to removing our skeleton from our body, taking away the tension of tendons and muscles hanging on bones, the tension of muscles pulling and pushing that make it possible for us to move about and work.

To remove this tension in our bodies would obviously be a big mistake. To do this in the biblical realm is a much greater mistake, for it is the tension of faith that keeps us in a biblical position, as we choose to believe truths we cannot fully understand—like the Trinity. We do not abandon our reason, but are tied primarily to Scripture rather than our logic. It is a place of humility, submitting our intellect, reason and emotions to the Word and trusting God to be able to put all those great truths together. It is not choosing one or the other, but both/and.

Point Illustrated

An example of this healthy biblical tension is what the Scripture says about Jesus. He is presented in the Word as the Lamb of God that takes away the sin of the world (Jn. 1:29; Rev. 5:6). And He is also presented as the Lion of the tribe of Judah (Rev. 5:5). These are very contradictory pictures, but they are both given in Scripture. Which is right? Which is true? Both, of course, are.

Humanly speaking we would tend to pick the one that appeals most to us and to ignore the other. Those aware of their sin and in need of comfort would tend to pick the Lamb. Those who are aggressive and action-oriented would tend to pick the Lion. However, we don't get to pick and choose: God has chosen for us and we must accept both these depictions and titles of Christ.

Jesus often had to deal with people who wanted to think in "either/or" terms rather than in "both/and" reality. The Pharisees and Herodians tried to trap Jesus with the question, "Is it lawful to pay taxes to Caesar or not?" They gave him two options; in their theology, one was clearly wrong, the other clearly right.

Jesus avoided the trap they had built for him—and themselves—by taking the question to a higher, wider level, a third possibility: "Render to Caesar the things that are Caesar's, and to God the things that are God's" (Mk. 12:13-17).

Leaving the theological box of the Pharisees, Jesus pointed out that both aspects are correct in their appropriate contexts. So it must be with us; we must rise above the boxes of theological black and white thinking, and let the multicolored, expansive realm of Scripture be our measure.

Chapter 2
How to String the Cable of Faith

The first step in bridging the gaps between seemingly contradictory truths is to look at all that Scripture has to say about a subject. We must be careful not to set up a straw man for a theological position that doesn't appeal to us; we must be honest and look at all that Scripture says.

A good place to practice this is the doctrine of the Trinity, the belief that God is one while He is also three persons. Humanly speaking this certainly sounds like a paradox: One while Three? We can't possibly understand this fully, but Scripture presents both truths, so we need to accept both.

To keep this presentation short, I'll use only a few references to illustrate each point of these two seemingly contradictory truths.

God is One

"Hear, O Israel: The LORD our God, *the LORD is one*" (Deu. 6:4).

"I am the LORD, and there is no other; *apart from me there is no God*" (Isa. 45:5; also Isa. 43:3; 44:8).

"The most important one [commandment]," answered Jesus, "is this: 'Hear, O Israel, the Lord our God, the *Lord is one*" (Mk. 12:29).

"A mediator, however, does not represent just one party; but *God is one*" (Gal. 3:20).

It is quite clear that our God is one.

God is Three

There are passages which show that the Father, Son and Holy Spirit are each a distinct person while also being God.

The first clue for this found in the first verse of the Bible: "In the beginning *God...*" (Gen. 1:1). The Hebrew word here translated as "God" is "Elohim," which in Hebrew is a plural, rather than the singular or dual ending, which are features of Hebrew; this points to three or more.

This is often referred to as the "plural of majesty." True. At the same time, while this is not "proof" of the Trinity, it is a hint, a foreshadowing from that beginning that God is not a simple one but a plurality. And the oneness of God is pointed out by the singular verb that often follows the plural noun "Elohim."

It is clear that the Father is God

"Do not work for food that spoils, but for food that endures to eternal life, which the Son of Man will give you. On him *God the Father* has placed his seal of approval" (Jn. 6:27; emphasis mine).

"Then the end will come, when he [Christ] hands over the kingdom to *God the Father* after he has destroyed all dominion, authority and power" (1Co. 15:24; see also Gal. 1:1; Eph. 5:20).

Jesus Christ is also God

A. Direct statements of Christ's divinity

"To those who through the righteousness of *our **God** and **Savior** Jesus Christ* have received a faith as precious as ours..." (2Pe. 1:1; emphasis mine).

"...Jesus our Lord. His *divine* power has given us everything we need for life and godliness..." (2Pe. 1:2,3; emphasis mine).

B. Jesus' claims to be God

"'We are not stoning you for any of these," replied the Jews, "but for blasphemy, because *you, a mere man, claim to be God*" (Jn. 10:33; also Jn. 5:17,18).

C. Others' declaration of Jesus being God.

"Thomas said to him, '*My Lord and my God!*'" (Jn. 20:28; emphasis mine)

D. Jesus is to be worshiped as God.

"...that all may *honor the Son just as they honor the Father*. He who does not honor the Son does not honor the Father, who sent him" (Jn. 5:23; emphasis mine).

E. Jesus' Titles are the same as God's

"I tell you the truth," Jesus answered, "before Abraham was born, *I am!*" (Jn. 8:58; emphasis mine)

*"I am the Alpha and the Omega, the First and the Last, the Beginning and the End...*I, Jesus, have sent my angel to give you this testimony for the churches" (Rev. 22:13,16; emphasis mine).

F. Jesus' Roles are the same as God's:

Jesus said, "I tell you the truth...*whatever the Father does the Son also does"* (Jn. 5:19; emphasis mine).

"...the Father judges no one, *but has entrusted all judgment to the Son..."* (Jn. 5:22; emphasis mine).

This short summary is enough to establish that Jesus Christ is God.

The Holy Spirit is also God

A. The Spirit participated in the creation: "In the beginning, God created the heavens and the earth. The earth was without form and void, and darkness was over the face of the deep. And the *Spirit of God* was hovering over the face of the waters" (Gen. 1:1,2; emphasis mine). The Spirit was there.

B. To lie to the Spirit is to lie to God: "Then Peter said, 'Ananias, how is it that Satan has so filled your heart that you have *lied to the Holy Spirit* and have kept for yourself some of the money you received for the land? Didn't it belong to you before it was sold? And after it was sold, wasn't the money at your disposal? What made you think of doing such a thing? *You have not lied to men but to God"* (Ac. 5:3-4; emphasis mine).

C. The Spirit is equated to God: "You, however, are controlled not by the sinful nature but *by the Spirit*, if *the Spirit of God* lives in you. And if anyone does not *have the Spirit of Christ*, he does not belong to Christ" (Rom. 8:9; emphasis mine).

"Where can I go from *your Spirit*? Where can I flee from your presence?" (Ps. 139:7; emphasis mine)

"No eye has seen…what God has prepared for those who love him" — but God has revealed it to us *by his Spirit*" (1Co. 2:10; emphasis mine).

"The Spirit searches all things, even the deep things of God. …no one knows the thoughts of God except *the Spirit of God*" (1Co. 2:9-11; emphasis mine).

"And he who searches our hearts knows *the mind of the Spirit*, because the Spirit intercedes for the saints in accordance with God's will" (Rom. 8:27; emphasis mine).

"There are different kinds of working, but the same God works all of them in all men. Now to each one the manifestation *of the Spirit* is given for the common good… *the same Spirit*…gives them to each one, just as he determines" (1 Cor. 12:6,7,11; emphasis mine).

D. The Holy Spirit has titles like Christ and does the work God.

"And it is the Spirit who testifies, because *the Spirit is the truth*" (1Jn. 5:6b; emphasis mine).

"…because through Christ Jesus the law of the *Spirit of life* set me free from the law of sin and death" (Rom. 8:2; emphasis mine).

"the Spirit himself *intercedes* for us with groans that words cannot express" (Rom. 8:26; emphasis mine).

"This is how you can recognize the *Spirit of God*: Every spirit that acknowledges that Jesus Christ has come in the flesh is from God…" (1Jn. 4:2; emphasis mine).

Verses that tie it all together

There are various places in Scripture where the all three Persons of the Trinity are presented together. In the first one below, both the concept of three persons and of one God are combined by having one name (singular) for all.

A. "Therefore go and make disciples of all nations, baptizing them *in the name of* the Father and of the Son and of the Holy Spirit" (Mat 28:19; emphasis mine).

B. "May the grace of the *Lord Jesus Christ*, and the love of

God, and the fellowship of *the Holy Spirit* be with you all" (2Co. 13:14).

C. Peter begins one of his letters with this three-part formula, showing how each member of the Trinity has specific roles: you "who have been chosen according to the foreknowledge of *God the Father*, through the sanctifying work of *the Spirit*, for obedience to *Jesus Christ* and sprinkling by his blood" (1 Peter 1:2).

D. Paul also shows the role of each in our salvation. "*God our Savior*…saved us…through the washing of rebirth and renewal by *the Holy Spirit*, whom he poured out on us generously through *Jesus Christ our Savior*…" (Tit. 3:4-6). Note that both God and Jesus are called "our Savior."

It is quite clear that here we have a "both/and" situation: *both* the truth that God is One, *and* that God is three persons. Both are taught in Scripture, hard as it is for us human beings to comprehend.

Sceptics have asked, how can one God be three? $1+1+1$ does not $=1$. Mathematically true. But to look at it a bit differently, $1 \times 1 \times 1$ does $= 1$! It's all a matter of seeing things from a proper perspective!

Why is the Trinity an important concept?

There are a multitude of reasons for the importance of this truth. I will mention only four here.

First, since God *is* love (it is not just a quality which He can have or not, love is His essence, something He always is), He must love. If He were just one being, He would need to create something to love. This would mean He was dependent on His creation, taking away from His divinity, His otherness. However, since there is fellowship and love amongst the three persons of the Trinity, God is entirely complete in Himself, with no need for any created being to love.

Second, because God is three, relationships and fellowship exists within the Godhead. So, when He made man in His image, He made human beings also as relational creatures, able to have a relationship with Him and with each other.

Third, the fact that God is both One and three puts Him beyond the concept of any human being. We cannot adequately understand this, meaning God is greater than any of His creatures. His Triuneness is a proof of His being God, totally other than we are.

Fourth, the Trinity made it possible for Jesus to become a man and die on the cross for our sins. If God were only one, who would keep the universe in place, listen to our prayers, and protect His children while He was confined to a body on earth, while he was nailed to the cross, while He was in the lower parts of the earth for 3 days? Being a Trinity makes all this possible.

Summary

Many of us grew up with this concept of the Trinity and haven't struggled too much with it—perhaps partly because we've never really thought much about it, just accepted it. Others who came to faith in Christ later in life have had to work it through as far as possible and then accept God's being a Trinity in faith, based on the biblical evidence He's given.

It is the acceptance of both sides of this truth—that God is one and that God is Three—that preserves the tension of truth, keeping us safe on God's network of faith, protecting us from heresy and syncretism. Those who reject the Trinity of God and choose one side or the other of this truth (either saying God is only one, or that God is actually three gods) are rejecting Scripture and are outside biblical, orthodox Christianity.

All true Christians have learned to accept that God is both One and Three. Although it is just not possible for a human mind to fully grasp how these two truths fit together, Scripture is clear: God is One, and God is three Persons. We are told to pray to the Father in the name of Jesus with the help of the Holy Spirit.

So, there's our example of how to string the cable of faith and then dwell out over the valley of the unknown. Difficult and uncomfortable at times, but a great opportunity to give God glory in living by faith. And remember, without faith it is impossible to please God (Hebrews 11:6).

Chapter 3
What Hampers Us in Stringing the Cables of Faith From One Side to the Other?

This chapter will present four hindrances that keep us from digging deeper when confronted with seemingly contradictory truths in the Bible.

Block Number One: We Avoid Discomfort

The first reason, very simply, is the desire to be comfortable. When I don't understand something, I am reluctant to accept it because it makes me uncomfortable. The tension of incomprehensible concepts make us restless.

Comfort is, I believe, the highest value for much of western civilization. How many times have you heard, or said yourself, "I can't do that—it's outside my comfort zone!" In our western cultures, feelings are supreme in evaluating possibilities. We don't ask what people think about things, we ask them, "how do you feel about that? Does it make you uncomfortable?"

As a result, comfort becomes the measure of what is good. Instead of wrestling with difficult issues, which is uncomfortable, we avoid them. Look at the "safe spaces" and "trigger announcements" that are so prevalent in universities today. Students can't stand anything that makes them uncomfortable.

So, when we are confronted with seemingly contradictory, seemingly irreconcilable concepts, our tendency is to do something to take away the tension: choose a side, ignore the other; stay only with those who agree with us; attack those who make us uncomfortable with their differentness. This prevents us from looking deeper into seemingly contradictory truths, keeps us from accepting both even when we can't fully comprehend them.

Block Number Two: Pride

When unsaved people are confronted with spiritual reality, pride is often a block to their accepting the truth of the Gospel. The concept of being a sinner, needing a Savior, of Jesus dying in their place, of His purchasing forgiveness for them with His blood and providing eternal life with His resurrection—all of this goes against human beings' natural grain. We would rather do it ourselves.

One speaker I heard, when asked why there are so many religions in the world, replied that there are actually only two. One, in many various forms, says that if we follow certain rules, we may become good enough to get into heaven. The other, Christianity, says that because we are sinners, we can't possibly do anything to redeem ourselves and need Jesus to save us.

The major aspect that holds people in the various versions of self-help religion and keeps many from considering the claims of Christ, is pride. They don't want to accept their neediness and would rather try to earn salvation on their own terms.

Pride also prevents us from accepting things that are difficult to fathom: "if I can't understand it, it is probably not true."

In contrast to this arrogance are David's words in Psalm 139:2-6. He could not understand how God can do all these things he mentions below, but accepted them by faith.

> *You know when I sit and when I rise;*
> *   you perceive my thoughts from afar.*
> *You discern my going out and my lying down;*
> *   you are familiar with all my ways.*
> *Before a word is on my tongue*
> *   you know it completely, O LORD.*
> *You hem me in—behind and before;*
> *   you have laid your hand upon me.*
> ***Such knowledge is too wonderful for me,***
> ***   too lofty for me to attain.*** (emphasis mine)

This is true humility—when we know but don't fully understand, and accept truth anyway. It is key to our growth as followers of Jesus Christ. Humility is the window to understanding; it is the door through which all grace comes: "God opposes the proud *but gives grace to the humble*" (Jas. 4:6; emphasis mine).

If we don't have the humility to admit that God knows better than us, to submit our intellect to His Word, accepting that He can put together seemingly opposing truths, then we are condemned to living in willful ignorance, spiritual poverty and bondage to pride.

Block Number Three:
The Quest for Importance and Security

The two things that everyone desires greatly are significance and security. Significance is normally sought through our achievements and other's opinions of us, as well as our possessions, power and position.

Security is something we seek through having control, keeping far from what we perceive to be danger and associating with people like us.

Some supposed sources of significance, such as achievement, power and position can also be gained vicariously, by joining a group such as a club, business or to be a fan of a sports team. When our group is successful, we partake of the sense of importance of that achievement.

Those who espouse a certain position, ideology or theology are also "joining" that group's perspective. They can become very committed to it and gain significance through being "right." They tend to believe they understand things better than others and therefore belong to an elite group, giving them both security and significance. Such an elitist attitude then prevents them from being open to any challenge which might threaten their sense of significance and security.

Look at the political and intellectual leftist elites today who look down on those poor deluded deplorables on the right. They are not willing to consider anything the other side thinks as valid and mock them for their values.

Those who have such an entrenched position will defend their cherished beliefs to the end, many times being unwilling to listen at all to "the other side." Their position is their emotional source of significance and to a degree their security. They have invested so much into this position that it is too costly to give it up.

You realized immediately, of course, that this is also a description of the Pharisees who opposed Jesus and his teaching, wanting to defend their privileged position. It is difficult to reason with such people, because their commitment is primarily emotional, not intellectual. No amount of sound reason can touch their emotional fortress.

A secular example of this is the commitment of the scientific community to evolution; they simply dismiss the possibility of creation, fully convinced that their way is the right one, period—no questions are to be asked!
In like manner, those strongly committed to theological positions like Calvinism or Armenianism, or any other position, tend to be closed to any penetrating dialogue on their theology. They are unwilling or unable to see either the deficiencies or the complimentary aspects of other positions.

Block Number Four: Greek Logic

The fourth reason for being unable or unwilling to research, discuss, comprehend or embrace seeming biblical paradoxes, is the influence of Greek logic as laid out by Aristotle and Plato.[3]

---

[3] Randy Alcorn in his book *Heaven* (Tyndale, 2004) on page 476 points to this unconscious influence of Greek thought in giving us a wrong impression of what Heaven will be like. He says, "Why are we so resistant to the idea that Heaven could be physical? The answer, I believe, is centered in an unbiblical belief that the spirit realm is good and the material world is bad, a view I am calling Christoplatonism.

"Plato, the Greek philosopher, believed that material things, including the human body and the earth, are evil, while immaterial things such as the soul and Heaven are good. This view is called Platonism. The Christian church, highly influenced by Platonism through the teachings of Philo (ca. 20 BC-AD 50) and Origen (AD 185 – 254), among others, came to embrace the "spiritual" view that human spirits are better off without bodies and that Heaven is a disembodied state. They rejected the notion of Heaven as a physical realm and spiritualized or entirely neglected the biblical teaching of resurrected people inhabiting a resurrected Earth.

"Christoplatonism has had a devastating effect on our ability to understand what Scripture says about Heaven, particularly about the eternal Heaven, the New Earth. A fine Christian man said to me, "This idea of having bodies and eating food and being in an earthly place... it just sounds so unspiritual". Without knowing it, he was under the influence of Christoplatonism. If we believe, even subconsciously, that bodies and the earth and material things are unspiritual, even evil, then we will inevitably reject or spiritualize any biblical revelation about our bodily resurrection or the

Professor Dr. Hans Rohrbach, a German mathematician and natural scientist, wrote about this in his article *Absolute Wahrheit?*[4] (*Absolute Truth?*). He pointed out that principles of Aristotle's logic have powerfully influenced much of our Western thinking and culture. This logic has become such a part of our worldview that we use Aristotle's principles unconsciously in our daily lives.

Here's how Dr. Rohrbach describes two of them.

1. *The law of non-contradiction: the idea that logically correct propositions cannot affirm and deny the same thing in the same way at the same time.*

This is, of course, valid: a man cannot be both an inveterate liar and honest at the same time. What is white cannot also be black. However, this principle tends to lock us into an either/or orientation where we are hampered from considering how *seemingly* contradictory statements *might* both be true. They may be two sides of the same coin, as Jesus pointed out in his reply to his questioners about paying taxes (render to God what is His, and to Caesar what is his).

Following the principle of non-contradiction can lead us to think it is unnecessary to examine seeming paradoxes in the Bible more closely.

2. *The principle of no third possibility,* also called the *law of excluded middle,* can be summarized as the idea that *every proposition must be either true or false, it cannot be both true and false, and it cannot be neither true nor false.*

This principle of logic, while valid, can also prevent us from considering or thinking through seemingly contradictory statements to see if they can be reconciled.

---

physical characteristics of the New Earth. That's exactly what has happened in most Christian churches, and it's a large reason for our failure to come to terms with a biblical doctrine of Heaven. Christoplatonism has also closed our minds to the possibility that the present Heaven may actually be a physical realm. If we look at Scripture, however, we'll see considerable evidence that the present Heaven has physical properties."

[4] Rhon Brief nr. 4 Dez. 1994, Christl. Tagungsstatte Hohe Rhon e.V. im Landesverband des CVJM Bayern, 97653 Bischofsheim, Deutschland.

For instance, if I told you that my father was my brother and that I married my sister, your first thought would probably be that my family had a severe morality problem.

But if you give me a chance to explain that I'm speaking of spiritual reality, and that all those who are born again are brothers and sisters in the family of God, that will completely change your perception. My father is not my brother physically, but spiritually; my wife is not my sister physically, but spiritually.

To think only in terms of the excluded middle again tends to lock our thinking into only two boxes (true or false), preventing us from gaining a possible wider understanding of how things could fit together.

This is demonstrated in John 11 where Jesus told his disciples that Lazarus' sickness would not end in death. They assumed, in normal human fashion, that there are just two possibilities in this situation, death or recovery; this led them to understand that he wouldn't die at all, and yet he did.

Jesus, on the other hand, was looking at the whole picture with a third possibility, and truly the story did not end in death—that was only a stop along the way—but in resurrection and a great burst of glory for God. Jesus gave an unexpected third possibility: life, death, then resurrection, all being true.

As a result of being steeped in this Aristotelian thinking, we are easily attracted to systems that strongly pick a position and defend it vigorously, not wanting to give any possibility of validity for any other position. One God, or three Persons. No room for the Trinity in this system. Yet, as we have seen, Scripture is clear that our Lord is both one God and three Persons![5]

---

[5] Richard Bauckham, in his book, *Jesus and the God of Israel* (Cambridge; Eerdmans, 2008, 80) writes about how Greek thought introduced ideas contrary to the OT understandings of God. "The earliest Christology was already the highest Christology. I call it a Christology of divine identity, proposing this as a way beyond the standard distinction between functional and ontic Christology, a distinction which does not correspond to early Jewish thinking about God and has, therefore, seriously distorted our understanding of New Testament Christology. When we think in terms of divine identity, rather than divine essence or nature, which are not the primary categories for Jewish theology we can see that the so-called divine functions which Jesus exercises are intrinsic to who God is. This Christology of divine identity is not a mere stage on the way to the patristic development ontological Christology in the

Professor Dr. Rohrbach goes on to say that scientists have shown that these rules of logic need to be complemented by other rules.

1. Along with the *law of non-contradiction (if two statements are contradictory, only one can be right, not both)* is the *principle of impartiality* where two seemingly contradictory things can both be true if we take the time to explore them.

A simple example of this is given by my daughter-in-law. She and her twin liked to tell people they were both twins and Cousins. That always brought a reaction, as biologically it is unlikely. If their parents were cousins, then you could possibly say the girls were both cousins and sisters. But for these girls there was another way that this was true: while they were born of the same mother and father, making them sisters, their last name was "Cousins," making them both sisters and Cousins, a truth not obviously evident in normal usage of these terms.

2. Along with the principle of *no third possibility, or the excluded middle*—which says that every proposition must be either true or false, it cannot be both true *and* false, and it cannot be neither true nor false—there is the *principle of complementarity.*

In explaining this, Dr. Rohrbach uses the example of light being made up of waves, and also of particles at the same time. Both are true because the waves themselves are made up of particles. Here is a third possibility where the two truths come together to complement each other.

John 1:1 gives us an illustration of the principle of complementarity: "In the beginning was the Word and the Word was with God and the Word was God."

To someone reading this for the first time, it sounds like nonsense, the Word being both with God and God himself. But when we understand the concept of the Trinity, it makes perfect sense. The Word is an entity by Himself and He is also God.

context of a Trinitarian theology. It is already a fully divine Christology, maintaining that Jesus Christ is intrinsic to the unique and eternal identity of God. The Fathers did not develop it so much as transpose it into a conceptional framework more concerned with the Greek philosophical categories of essence and nature."

In a third example, Dr. Rohrbach points out that the Bible speaks of a visible and an invisible world, both of which exist at the same time. It is not one or the other, but both.

The Bible presents the reality of both worlds, making these complementary truths. As natural human beings, we live in a visible world, but at the same time, as spiritual beings, we live in an invisible world where we have a soul and spirit, and there are angels, demons and the hand of God. Think of the servant of Elisha having his eyes opened so he could see the army of God surrounding the army of Arameans (2 Kings 6:17).

In addition, in this unseen world we can have two seemingly contradictory truths existing side by side, such as a born-again person having two natures (Gal. 5:16,17). These two worlds are not contradictory but complementary.

So, Dr. Rohrbach's insights can help to free us from the tendency of being tied to either/or thinking.[6]

In the debates between Calvinism and Arminianism that have gone on for centuries, both sides seem to have been

---

[6] Randy Alcorn, in his book *Heaven*, gives other examples of Greek philosophical thought influencing Christianity. "Prior to the Middle Ages, people thought of Heaven tangibly – as a city or a paradise garden, as portrayed in Scripture. But the writings of twelfth-century theologians such as Peter Abelard and Peter Lombard and thirteenth-century theologian Thomas Aquinas led to the philosophical movement known as scholasticism, which came to dominate medieval thought and ultimately took hostage the doctrine of Heaven.

The scholastic writers viewed Heaven in a much more impersonal, cold, and scientific manner than their predecessors. They departed from the Heaven of Scripture that contains both the unfamiliar transcendent presence of God, surrounded by the cherubim, and familiar earthly objects and personages, including people wearing clothes and having conversations. They embraced a Heaven entirely intangible, immaterial, and hence – they thought – more spiritual. They claimed that heaven couldn't be made of familiar elements such as earth, water, air, and fire. Instead, the argued, "the empyrean (the highest heaven or heavenly sphere) must be made of a fifth and nobler element, the quintessence, which must be something like pure light. And they ignored almost entirely – or allegorized into oblivion – the New Earth as the eternal dwelling place of resurrected humans living with resurrected Jesus in a physical realm of natural wonders, physical structures, and cultural distinctives.

The scholastic view gradually replaced the old, more literal understanding of Heaven as garden and city, a place of earthly beauty, dwelling places, food, and fellowship. The loss was incalculable. The church to this day has never recovered from the unearthly – and anti-earthly – theology of Heaven constructed by well-meaning but misguided scholastic theologians. These men interpreted biblical revelation not in a straightforward manner, but in light of the intellectually seductive notions of Platonism, Stoicism, and Gnosticism.

hampered by a stilted application of Aristotle's logic. One side comes down hard on God's sovereignty and the other on the free will of man: for them it's either/or, no possibility of a third way.

A Call to Consider

So, I encourage us all to lay aside what blocks us from considering both sides of the great Truths of the Word. These blocks include the following.

- Our commitment to comfort: not wanting to disturb our peace by examining our presuppositions in the light of new information and perspectives.

- Our persistent pride in being sure we are right and there's nothing more to be considered, so we close up to any real dialogue.

- Our deep desire for significance and security, not wanting to reexamine our positions that make us feel important and in control.

- Our unconscious dependence on a faulty application of Greek logic, leaving us closed to third possibilities.

Let us be humble and honest in our look at Scripture—that is, being willing to see what it says, seeming contradictions and all, without the preconceptions of our theological systems.

This means taking into consideration all aspects, including those seeming paradoxes and those statements that don't fit into our assumptions. Such openness and intellectual honesty are key, as such positions are the demonstration of true humility—submitting our intellect to God's Word.

An example of this is found in John 9:2 where the disciples asked Jesus concerning the blind man, "'Rabbi, who sinned, this man or his parents, that he was born blind?'" Jesus' answer took them out of their either/or thinking, common to their culture, to a wider perspective, a third alternative. "'Neither this man nor his parents sinned,' said Jesus, 'but this happened so that the works of God might be displayed in him.'"

Following Jesus' example of thinking in full-orbed fashion could lead us to a balanced, biblical stance that resolves the theological conundrums both sides have had to contend with over the centuries. We will look at some of these in the next chapters.

As Jesus said, in His great high priestly prayer to His Father, "I have given them the glory that you gave me, that they may be one as we are one—I in them and you in me—*so that they may be brought to complete unity. Then the world will know that you sent me* and have loved them even as you have loved me" (Jn. 17:22,23; emphasis mine).

Chapter 4
Bridging the Gap

Here is a brief summary of the differences between Arminianism and Calvinism concerning man's role in salvation. The first part is from the website www.graceonline.library.org

ARMINIANISM Free Will or Human Ability	CALVINISM Total Inability or Total Depravity
Although human nature was seriously affected by the fall, man has not been left in a state of total spiritual helplessness. God graciously enables every sinner to repent and believe, but He does not interfere with man's freedom…. The lost sinner needs the Spirit's assistance, but he does not have to be regenerated by the Spirit before he can believe. for faith is man's act and precedes the new birth.	Because of the fall, man is unable of himself to savingly believe the gospel. The sinner is dead, blind, and deaf to the things of God; his heart is deceitful and desperately corrupt
Each sinner possesses a free will, and his eternal destiny depends on how he uses it. Man's freedom consists of his ability to choose good over evil in spiritual matters; his will is not enslaved to his sinful nature.	. His will is not free, it is in bondage to his evil nature, therefore, he will not — indeed he cannot — choose good over evil in the spiritual realm. Consequently, it takes much more than the Spirit's assistance to bring a sinner to Christ —it takes regeneration by which the Spirit makes the sinner alive and gives him a new nature

Faith is the sinner's gift to God; it is man's contribution to salvation The sinner has the power to either cooperate with God's Spirit and be regenerated or resist God's grace and perish	Faith is not something man contributes to salvation but is itself a part of God's gift of salvation— it is God's gift to the sinner, not the sinner's gift to God
ELECTION	ELECTION
Conditional Election – God only "chooses" those whom He knows will choose to believe. No one is predetermined for either heaven or hell.	Unconditional election: Because man is dead in sin, he is unable to initiate a response to God; therefore, in eternity past God elected certain people to salvation.
Conditional election states that God elects individuals to salvation based on His foreknowledge of who will believe in Christ unto salvation, thereby on the condition that the individual chooses God.[7]	Election and predestination are unconditional; they are not based on man's response because man is unable to respond, nor does he want to.[8] God elects individuals to salvation based entirely on His will, not on anything inherently worthy in the individual

As you can see, Arminians give strong emphasis to the role of man in salvation. They believe in his ability to provide faith, his ability to choose good over evil in the spiritual as well as physical relm and his responsibility to respond to the gospel.

Calvinists take the opposite tact, giving total emphasis to God's role to bring regeneration through irresistible grace before a person can believe, basically discounting man's active involvement altogether.

If we look at the Bible as a whole, we certainly find many references to both of these aspects. Here are four examples of each.

---

[7] Quoted from https://www.gotquestions.org/Calvinism-vs-Arminianism.html

[8] Quoted from https://www.gotquestions.org/calvinism.html, a four point Calvinist website

Man's role

"For we also have had the gospel preached to us, just as they did; but the message they heard was of no value to them, because those who heard *did not combine it with faith*" (Heb. 4:2; emphasis mine). They made a choice.

"Whoever believes in him is not condemned, but whoever *does not believe* stands condemned already *because they have not believed* in the name of God's one and only son" (Jn. 3:18; emphasis mine). Again, a choice was made.

Jesus said, "So I say to you: *Ask* and it will be given to you; *seek* and you will find; *knock* and the door will be opened to you" (Lk. 11:9; emphasis mine). We must choose to ask.

"When Jesus spoke again to the people, he said, "I am the light of the world. *Whoever follows me* will never walk in darkness, but will have the light of life" (Jn. 8:12; emphasis mine). A choice is required from whoever.

God's total sovereignty

"*Whatever the Lord pleases He does*, in heaven and in earth, in the seas and in all deep places" (Psa. 135:6; emphasis mine).

"The LORD *foils* the plans of the nations; he *thwarts* the purposes of the peoples. But the plans of the LORD stand firm forever, the purposes of his heart through all generations" (Ps. 33:10,11; emphasis mine).

"...*God has mercy on whom he wants* to have mercy, and *he hardens whom he wants* to harden...For *God has bound everyone over to disobedience* so that he may have mercy *on them all*" (Rom. 9:18; 11:32; emphasis mine).

Jesus said, "And I, when I am lifted up from the earth, *will draw all people to myself*" (Jn. 12:32; emphasis mine).

Our tendency in reading these seemingly contradictory presentations is to immediately go to the "either/or" of Aristotle's logic and say, "They can't both be right; it's either one or the other, either God is totally sovereign or man has the ability to choose." Then we will try to reinterpret the biblical statements we don't like in the light of the ones we accept.

However, when both of these seemingly exclusive points are

included by God in His Word, we need to reject our natural human reasoning and diligently study how God, in His much higher ways, thinks.

We need to remember that two seemingly contradictory things can both be true, giving us a third alternative, even in the physical world. As said before, light is made up of waves and light is made up of particles. And these two truths are easily united in a third alternative: light is made up of waves which are made up of particles. So, we need to affirm that it is possible to have a third alternative in this theological disagreement, too.

The Paradox of Suffering

Another example of our difficulty as human beings to grasp the expanse of God's wisdom is seen in His promises on one side to protect from suffering, and on the other, the suffering He allows.

Psalm 91:9,10 (ESV) says, "Because You have made the LORD Your dwelling place—the Most High, who is my refuge— no evil shall be allowed to befall you, no plague come near your tent."

But what about Job? He was a man who made God his refuge, yet suffered great tragedy, heartache, sickness, pain and distress—a suffering compounded by both his wife and his "friends." Isn't this harm and evil and a plague?

We must turn to God and the rest of His Word to grasp a bigger, higher and wider view of things. I'll mention just two balancing truths, although there are more.

First is that God's understanding of harm or evil is different than ours. Evil or harm is not what makes us uncomfortable or disappointed or gives pain and loss, but transgression of His commands, by us or others, that damages us spiritually, what drives us away from God.

As it says in Romans 8:35,37, even in the midst of great trouble, we are still in God's love: "Who shall separate us from the love of Christ? Shall trouble or hardship or persecution or famine or nakedness or danger or sword?" Such things do come to believers with God's permission, but in them we are still in His love. "No, in all these things we are more than conquerors through him who loved us."

As we make Him our refuge, He is always there to protect us from true spiritual harm: "Because he holds fast to me in love, I will deliver him; I will protect him, because he knows my name. When he calls to me, I will answer him; I will be with him in trouble; I will rescue him and honor him" (Ps. 91:14,15; ESV). This is just what God did for Abraham, Joseph, David, Daniel, Paul—and Jesus—in the midst of all their troubles and suffering.

The Father let Jesus go through worse suffering than any other person ever experienced, because He and Jesus both had a higher purpose: securing salvation for all human beings. Then the Father rescued Jesus from death and honored Him. So He does with us when He has a higher purpose for our suffering.

Second, suffering, difficulty and loss all are tools God uses for multiple purposes, such as: to mature us (James 1:2-4),[9] to give us opportunity to earn rewards Matthew 5:11,12),[10] and to give us a wider platform to be a witness and glory-giver for Him (Php. 1:12,13).[11]

We can see all three of these elements at work in Job's suffering. In the end, God did not answer Job's question of "why," but just said, "Trust me! I have a purpose you can't see yet."

Job chose to trust and was able to give God much glory by his faith. He was deepened and matured by his trials and has become the measure of suffering, of faith and of comfort for millions over the years.

What he went through was horrendous, but it was not harm or evil in the biblical sense of those words, driving him away from God. Harm and evil are the result of decisions like Adam

---

[9] "Consider it pure joy, my brothers and sisters, whenever you face trials of many kinds, because you know that the testing of your faith produces perseverance. Let perseverance finish its work so that you may be mature and complete, not lacking anything" (Jas. 1:2-4)

[10] "Blessed are you when people insult you, persecute you and falsely say all kinds of evil against you because of me. Rejoice and be glad, because great is your reward in heaven, for in the same way they persecuted the prophets who were before you" (Mt. 5:11,12).

[11] "Now I want you to know, brothers and sisters, that what has happened to me has actually served to advance the gospel. As a result, it has become clear throughout the whole palace guard and to everyone else that I am in chains for Christ" (Php. 1:12,13).

and Eve's or king Saul's in rebellion or David's in committing adultery.

This view of suffering is very different from our normal human understanding, giving us a third alternative to our natural "good" and "evil" categories: God bring good out of suffering, making suffering useful rather than evil being random, meaningless events.

An Analogy

Such seeming conflicts as the paradox of God's promises and allowed suffering, and especially the seeming paradox of God's sovereignty and man's responsibility, remind me of a zipper. One side of a zipper by itself isn't of much use beyond decoration. In fact, we would call one side alone useless. It's only when the two sides are joined together by the proper mechanism that a zipper is functional and useful.

In one example of my little analogy here, one side of the zipper is that God is One; the other is that God is Three. Both are there in the Bible and both are true; and as we know, they are joined by the statement every true Christian accepts, that God is One in essence and God is three in persons.

In the subject we are considering here, one side of the zipper is the Calvinist position, the other is the Arminian.

The zipper mechanism needed to join the Calvinist and Arminian sides together is the Bible itself. A good, unbiased reading of the Bible, giving a healthy overview of Scripture, as well as careful attention to the details, will bring the points of the two sides together, giving a third alternative by joining the work of God with the responsibility of man.

The Arminian Side of the Zipper

The Arminians believe that, "God graciously enables every sinner to repent and believe."

I affirm that this is true, as Jesus said, "...no one can come to me unless the Father has enabled him" (Jn. 6:65), along with the truth that, "God our Savior…wants all people to be saved and to come to a knowledge of the truth" (1Ti. 2:4).

The Bible also affirms that people, left in their natural, depraved state, will not seek God, and cannot seek Him. "There is no one who understands, no one who seeks God." (Rom. 3:11) And without His enabling, we cannot respond, "…the sinful mind is hostile to God. It does not submit to God's law, nor can it do so" (Rom. 8:7).

Therefore, God, after providing salvation, declares that He wants everyone to respond to His offer. "The Lord is not slow in keeping his promise, as some understand slowness. Instead he is patient with you, *not wanting anyone to perish, but everyone to come to repentance*" (2Pe. 3:9; emphasis mine).

And, "…we have put our hope in the living God, who is the Savior of *all* people [He has provided all that is needed for all], and *especially* of *those who believe*" [but only those who choose to believe are actually saved] (1Ti. 4:10; emphasis mine).

So, God takes the initiative to make it possible for people to believe and be born again. As Jesus said in John 6:65, "…I told you that no one can come to me unless the Father has enabled them."

Here are some of the things God does to give us sinners the possibility to believe, to enable us to believe.

- He reveals Himself through creation in a way so that people can understand this revelation. "For since the creation of the world, God's invisible qualities—his eternal power and divine nature—*have been clearly seen, being understood* from what has been made, *so that men are without excuse*" (Rom. 1:20; emphasis mine).

- He gives light to each person. "The true light that *gives light to every man* was coming into the world" (Jn. 1:9; emphasis mine).

- He gives conviction through the Holy Spirit to bring realization of guilt to everyone in the world. "Unless I go away, the Counselor will not come to you; but if I go, I will send him to you. When he comes, *he will convict the world[12]* of guilt in regard to sin and righteousness and judgment..." (Jn. 16:7-8; emphasis mine).

- He works to bring cooperation in removing spiritual blindness ("the veil"): "But whenever anyone turns to the Lord [responding to God's work above], *the veil is taken away*" (2Co. 3:16; emphasis mine).

- He causes the light of the gospel to shine into hearts. "For God, who said, 'Let light shine out of darkness,' *made his light shine in our hearts* to give us the light of the knowledge of the glory of God in the face of Christ" (2Co. 4:6; emphasis mine).

- He "pins people down," putting them in positions where they have to face their need for a Savior. Psalm 107 gives four examples of this. God also did this with king Nebuchadnezzar, giving him a time of insanity; He did this with Saul when Jesus appeared to him on the road to Damascus and made him blind for a while; He did this with me, putting me into a corner where I had to face my inability to handle life on my own.

- Through Scripture God repeatedly calls all sinners to repent and believe. "Come to me, *all you who are weary and burdened,* and I will give you rest" (Mt. 11:28). Jesus himself said in John 12:32, "And I, when I am lifted up from the earth, will draw *all* people to myself" (emphasis mine).

- God is also very active in the world today revealing Himself to unbelievers through means appropriate to each one's culture, including dreams and visions, giving them Scriptural Truth in places where there is no possibility of them hearing the Gospel from other people, and thereby leading them to those who can share the good news with them.[13]

---

[12] Some Calvinists have told me that here the word "world" (Greek *"kosmos"*) actually means the elect. But there is no linguistic basis for this. They must try and change the meaning of the Greek word in order to remain consistent in their theological system, a definitely dangerous move.

[13] In working for 33 years in the Middle East with Muslims, I found that almost every person I met who had become a born-again believer in Jesus Christ, had a dream about Jesus as part of the process of coming to belief.

In relation to this last point, it is significant to note that the word "whoever" (occurring 183 times in the Bible) is used often in God's call to believe. This word includes everyone: "For God so loved the world that he gave his one and only Son, that *whoever* believes in him shall not perish but have eternal life" (John 3:16). And in John 7:35, "Then Jesus declared, 'I am the bread of life. *Whoever* comes to me will never go hungry, and whoever believes in me will never be thirsty.'" The passage goes on to show the interweaving of God's enabling and people's responsibility to believe. "Whoever" means whoever—anyone willing to respond![14]

Concerning election, Arminians believe that as God offers salvation to all, He knows that all will not respond. And also He knows who will respond. Those are the ones He makes sure will have all that is needed to come to faith.

As it says in Romans 8:29-30 "For those God *foreknew* he also predestined to be conformed to the image of his Son that he might be the firstborn among many brothers and sisters. And those he predestined, he also called; those he called, he also justified; those he justified, he also glorified." Note the progression, first foreknew, then predestined.

And in 1 Peter 1:2 it says, "To God's elect ... who have been chosen according to the foreknowledge of God the Father...." He chose them in line with what He knew ahead of time, that they would respond to His invitation. This point is given more in depth discussion in chapter 13, as well as a bit further on in this chapter.

As we continue thinking about the Arminian side of the zipper, it is important to point out that their statement about faith is *not* biblical. They say, "Faith is the sinner's gift to God; it is man's contribution to salvation".

However, in Romans 10:17 the Bible states, "Consequently, *faith comes from hearing the message*, and the message is heard through the word of Christ" (emphasis mine). We are called to join God in the process by reading the Word, but faith *comes* from that reading and hearing, it is not something that we can

---

[14] Some Calvinists have said that "whosoever" means the elect, but that is an assumption to fit their theology, not a biblically or linguistically verifiable fact, see above on how God enables all to come to Him.

produce and give to God.

Also, in 2 Peter 1:2, it says, "To those who through the righteousness of our God and Savior Jesus Christ *have received a faith* as precious as ours…" (emphasis mine). Biblical faith is something that we receive, not provide.

The Calvinist Side of the Zipper

The Calvinists are correct in their keeping the sovereignty of God and the depravity of man on center stage, and it is right to make this a trinity by adding man's responsibility. As we saw above, only if God acts in His Sovereignty to help people can they believe.

However, to strengthen their position that unregenerate man is totally incapable of responding to the gospel, some Calvinists use the analogy of a corpse to illustrate the truth of the depravity of man. They say that each unsaved person is "dead, blind and deaf." No matter what you say to a corpse or do to it, it cannot respond.

Therefore, they conclude that an unregenerate person must first be "regenerated," born again, before he can believe. As quoted above, they say, "It takes much more than the Spirit's assistance to bring a sinner to Christ—it takes regeneration by which the Spirit makes the sinner alive and gives him a new nature." [15]

As said, there is truth to their assertion that sinful man is not capable of responding to the gospel on his own, but it is not all the truth. Unbelievers are not like a corpse. Analogies are not the Word of God.

In fact, even Arthur Pink, an extreme Calvinist, recognized the fallacy of the corpse analogy: "A corpse in the cemetery is not a suitable analogy of the natural man. A corpse in the cemetery is incapable of performing evil! A corpse cannot 'despise and reject' Christ (Isaiah 53:3), cannot 'resist the Holy Spirit' (Acts 7:51), cannot disobey the gospel (2 Thes. 1:8); but the natural man can and does these things!"[16]

---

[15] Edwin H. Palmer, *The Five Points of Cavinism* (Baker Books, enlarged ed. 20th printing, 1999).

[16] Arthur W. Pink, *Studies in the Scriptures* (n.p. 1927) 250-261

Here are other points to consider in rejecting this analogy. First, the biblical depiction of spiritual death is not total inability of the whole person, but a separation. Physical death is when the spirit and soul leave the body, but the spirit and soul (the actual person) do not cease to function. Spiritual death is *not* when people are made incapable of interacting with God, but it is when they are separated from a relationship with God, as Adam and Eve were after they sinned in the Garden.

All through the Bible there are examples of God interacting with sinners, even though they are "dead" spiritually and separated from Him by sin. Think of the conversation God had with Adam and Eve right after they first sinned and died spiritually. In spite of this, they were able to hear and respond to God as He talked with them.

Think of how God talked with Cain both before and after Cain killed his brother. 1 John 3:12 tells us, "Do not be like Cain, *who belonged to the evil one* and murdered his brother." Clearly Cain was not a believer, yet he could interact with God.

As mentioned above, God gives, through His creation, the witness of His existence and character to all people. The Bible is clear that people can understand this, even though they are spiritually dead (separated from God): "For since the creation of the world God's invisible qualities—his eternal power and divine nature—*have been clearly seen, being understood* from what has been made, *so that men are without excuse*" (Rom 1:20). We are without excuse because unregenerate people can see, hear and understand.[17]

This does not mean this is enough for all to believe—as we have shown—for to do so requires more help from God and each person must make his/her own decision. But they have no

---

[17] While I was teaching school in 1968 in an Eskimo village on an island close to Siberia, I met a 78-year-old Eskimo who was a follower of Jesus Christ. He told how he had grown up in Siberia as a shamanist, that is a demon worshiper, far from God with no chance to hear the gospel. The demons, he said, told them they'd created the world. He did not accept this, however, because the beauty of the world stood in stark contrast to the evil and ugly things the demons did. "There must be a good creator God," said my friend to himself. Then as a teenager he joined a hunting trip to the island where we met many years later. There he met a believer who opened his Bible, telling him of Jesus. "Aha," said my friend, "This is the good creator God I've been seeking!" and he accepted Christ, becoming a born-again believer. God was able to speak to an unregenerate, uninformed man through the creation and then provide what was needed for him to come to belief.

excuse; they are responsible because they can understand that God exists and is powerful, faithful and good.

So, although people are naturally dead spiritually, God does and can interact with them as part of the process of bringing them to salvation.

The Calvinists are also correct in their summary of Calvinist doctrine quoted above, saying that, "God elects individuals to salvation based…not on anything inherently worthy in the individual." We are fully unworthy of His salvation, and it is only His full grace that makes it possible to be saved and to accept His offer of salvation. Our acceptance of His offer does not infer that we have any innate worth, but simply accept His offer grace as He has enabled us.

God Sovereignly Gives Spheres of Influence

The Calvinists are right: God *is* totally sovereign. He is the great and final authority for all. It is possible that God, being fully sovereign, could be the primary and sole cause of everything that happens. He could control every decision, every event, every detail of our lives, making all decisions for us, leaving us no latitude for any personal or responsible action or decision. He could be such a God—except that He has told us otherwise in His revealed Word, commanding us to make real decisions in many areas of life, such as, "Seek first the Kingdom of God….".

The Arminians are also right: man *is* able to make moral and ethical choices (Luke 11:13 "If you then, who are evil, know how to give good gifts to your children…").

In Scripture we see that God, in His sovereignty, has chosen to give each human being a sphere of influence where they can make such real moral and ethical decisions.

In the biblical narrative, God gives commands and people obey or disobey. The Old Testament is full of people who obeyed (Abraham, Joseph and Daniel) and those who didn't (Cain, Saul and Jezebel). In His sovereignty, He allowed both.

Concerning election, Calvinists insist that God cannot know anything unless He predestines it; this belief flows not from Scriptural truth but from their definition of God's Sovereignty, something they feel compelled to defend. This subject is given greatly expanded treatment in the second portion of this book, so please look there if you want further explanation.

In actuality, Calvinists have a weak view of God here, limiting His knowing to only what He predetermines. If He is truly all knowing, He would certainly know ahead of time all the decisions of every person, as well as their outcomes, without having to make all these decisions for them.

This is made clear in Luke 7:30 "But the Pharisees and the experts in the law *rejected* God's purpose for themselves ..." (emphasis mine). God had a purpose for them, His will for them, but these men were able to reject it. This is not what God wanted; He did not predestine these men to reject His will, but they were able chose to do so.

God knew this would happen; He does not need to predestine to foreknow. On tiny scale, it is like my knowing what my son will do if I put a plate of eggplant before him: he will reject it. I do not predetermine that, but I know my son's preferences and can thereby know what his response will be.

In light of their concept of election, Calvinists take Romans 8:29, "For those God foreknew he also predestined..." to say that in foreknowing, He predetermined who would become believers. They are in effect saying this verse means "For those God predestined, he predestined."

However, taking this verse at face value brings a different conclusion. To foreknow simply means to know ahead of time—there is no linguistic or contextual reason to say it means to predetermine; the only reason to give it that interpretation is to make it fit into the overall doctrinal position of the Calvinists that God cannot know what He does not predetermine.

In a straightforward reading, God, knowing who will believe, predestines that they will have the opportunity to believe and be conformed to the image of Christ. This subject is given much more in-depth treatment in chapters 12 and 13.

In giving man the responsibility to make ethical and moral decisions, God has sovereignly limited his Sovereignty. He does this in a multitude of areas.

Whenever He makes a promise, He ties Himself to that point. For instance, Jesus was designated the Savior before the world was made: God limited Himself to this one solution.

When God called Abraham, He limited Himself, by His

promises to Abraham, to working through the Jews to bring the Savior. He limited Himself to working through Judah, then through David and his descendants to bring the Messiah into the world.

This sovereign limiting of His sovereignty is God's prerogative: "Whatever the Lord pleases He does…" (Ps. 135:6).

God Loves Partnership

God is also at work calling people to partner with Him, encouraging them to join Him in what He is doing. All through Scripture we see this pattern: God in His sovereignty prepares situations and people, both believers and unbelievers, then calls for them to join Him in his plans, giving them the option to say yes or no.

Luke 7:30 shows that people, in their God-given ability to make ethical and moral decisions, can reject the working of the Spirit. "But the Pharisees and experts in the law *rejected God's purpose for themselves…*" (emphasis mine).

The whole book of Proverbs is based on the possibility of people choosing to obey God or not, to be wise or to be fools. This, of course, is what we see throughout the whole Bible

When people respond to God's desire and cooperate, God takes the next step. When people fail to respond, there are negative consequences and God waits for them to repent, encouraging them to do so. Here are some examples.

- After creation, Adam was told to name the animals, joining God in the creative process. He was told till the land and cultivate the garden, joining God in the care of His creation; this he did. Adam was also told to avoid just one point of disobedience. He chose, instead, to rebell, resulting in his fall, which brought the whole human race into sin and warped the whole universe. This decision was the opposite of God's stated will.

- Noah was instructed to build the ark in God's detailed and specific way, joining God in His plan to save Noah and his family. He did this in the face of much opposition and preserved the human race along with every type of land animal. All the other people refused to respond to Noah's preaching and example, and therefore perished.

- Abraham was invited to follow God's call to leave home and join God in His plan to establish a nation in the land of Canaan. And he obeyed, not knowing where he was going.

- Abraham was told he would have a son by Sarah, but instead of waiting for God's timing, followed his wife's culturally-based advice and brought about a painful situation for the whole world.

- After being sold by his jealous older brothers, Joseph was able to forgive them and to embrace God's plan to send him to Egypt so he could develop his administrative talents, as seen in Joseph's being a willing servant to Potiphar and the prison warden. We know he forgave his brothers because bitter, angry people don't readily serve others. Joseph thereby became the savior of his family and surrounding countries—and eventually part of our salvation by saving his brother Judah, from whom came the Christ.

- Moses was prepared by his time as a shepherd in the wilderness and then was called at the burning bush to deliver Israel from slavery in Egypt. But he didn't want the assignment; he only agreed after God carefully and persistently persuaded him to go.

- God told Moses to speak to the rock so water would gush out, but Moses instead followed his anger and struck the rock, thereby stealing glory from God and was excluded from entering the promised land.

- Saul was called to lead Israel as her first king and to walk in obedience to God's laws and commands. However, he repeatedly disobeyed, and therefore was, in the end, rejected.

- David was called to serve Saul in preparation to be king. This he did, despite Saul's repeated attacks on his life, refusing twice to take the opportunity to kill Saul. David chose to obey God and opened the way for God's promise to be fulfilled in his becoming king in God's time and way.

- David was called to live an exemplary life as king, but in disobedience to God, committed both adultery and murder to satisfy himself, thereby bringing trouble on his family and the nation.

- Jonah was called to go and warn Nineveh of God's impending judgment, but, as you know, went the other way. God, using great creativity, convinced him to repent and go to Nineveh. Then when Jonah preached, the Ninevites repented and God withheld his judgment, much to Jonah's distress. God then worked with Jonah to bring him out his anger and self-pity, but there is no indication that Jonah repented.

- In a later repeat of this with another prophet, the Ninevites refused to believe and repent, so were destroyed.

- Daniel was called to stand up for the truth of God's laws and to be His witness in the face of repeated dangers, resulting eventually in king Nebuchadnezzar becoming a believer and calling his whole Empire to worship the true God.

- This pattern continues through to today as people are called to respond to the work of the Holy Spirit to accept the salvation that God has provided.

Calvinists, Arminians and Jesus

The Calvinist position, in their own words is, "Because of the fall, man is unable of himself to savingly believe the gospel." As we have said, this is true. We are unable in and of ourselves to seek God, believe or be saved in our own strength.

The Arminian position, as quoted above says, "God graciously enables every sinner to repent and believe...." This also is true, for God has prepared everything needed for salvation; and He gives people multiple forms of help (as we saw above on pages 44 and 45) so they are able to believe "savingly," if they are willing.

Calvinists also correctly state that "Faith is not something man contributes to salvation," and add that it is "God's gift to the sinner, not the sinner's gift to God." This is true; we receive our faith ("To those who through the righteousness of our God and Savior Jesus Christ *have received a faith* as precious as ours" 2 Pet. 1:1b). It is also true that faith is something we must cooperate in receiving by being willing to hear ("So then faith comes by hearing, and hearing by the word of God" – Rom. 10:17).

On the Calvinist side, there is strong objection to any hint of including a role for people in the salvation process, for in the Calvinistic system, God does it all. In adherence to Aristotle's either/or logic, the only option they can see for anyone who does not fully accept the Calvinist position, is to be an Arminian.

However, there is a third way, another position. Jesus Himself shows this by joining the work of God and the responsibility of man in salvation with one clear statement. When the crowd asked him, "'What must we do to do the works God requires?'"

"Jesus answered, '*The work* of God is this: *to believe* in the one he has sent'" (Jn. 6:28,29; emphasis mine). This is what God expects of mankind, a response to what God has prepared.

The Apsotle John agrees with the need to join God by acting in obedience, "And this is his command: to believe in the name of his Son, Jesus Christ…" (1Jn. 3:23).

Calvinist D.A. Carson also agrees, "God's unconditional sovereignty and the responsibility of human beings are mutually compatible."[18]

And, amazingly enough, Calvin himself agrees with this in his commentary on John 12:47 "And if any man hear my words, and believe not, I judge him not: for I came not to judge the world, but to save the world."

---

[18] D.A. Carson, *The Difficult Doctrine of the Love of God* (Crossway Books, 2000), 52.

Calvin writes: "For He delayed pronouncing judgement on them because He had come rather *for the salvation of all*...Because He had temporarily laid aside the office of judge and *offers salvation to all indiscriminately* and stretches out His arms *to embrace all, that all may* be the more encouraged to repent. And yet He heightens by an important detail the crime of rejecting an invitation so kind and gracious; for it is as if He had said: 'See, *I have come to call all*; and forgetting the role of judge, my one aim is to attract and rescue from destruction those who already seem doubly ruined.' Hence no man is condemned for despising the Gospel save he who *spurns* the lovely news of salvation *and deliberately decides to bring destruction on himself.*"[19]

So, in light of the above, especially Calvin's own words, God readied all for the potential salvation of all, sending the Savior and then working in the hearts of people, (as detailed above), giving them all that is necessary for them to believe, including granting faith and repentance. It is then the responsibility of people to respond to the work of the Trinity in their lives by believing "in the one he has sent."

This is not adding anything to salvation, any more than reaching out and taking a gift adds to the cost or work of the one who is giving it. We are invited to respond to God's offer of forgiveness and salvation, and can do so because He has given us all the help we need.

---

[19] Calvin's Commentary on John 12:47, emphases mine. Note that Calvin here, in his later and more mature writings, contradicts the doctrines of limited atonement, total depravity and unconditional election!

Chapter 5
Putting It All Together

Zipping things up with the Word of God provides a "third way," taking the truth within Calvinism and the truth within Arminianism, and joining them to give us the full-orbed picture we see in Scripture.

On one side, we have the Sovereignty of God; on the other side we have the moral responsibility of man, which God in His Sovereignty has granted.

God knew that Adam would sin, and allowed it, but definitely did not cause it. How could a holy God, who abhors sin, cause Adam to choose what God had forbidden? As James 1:13 clearly tells us, "…God cannot be tempted by evil, nor does he tempt anyone…."

God prepared a way of salvation through Christ; in addition, as we have seen, He then does all that is necessary so human beings can respond, giving them sight, light, conviction, revelation, faith, repentance and confrontation.

He calls everyone to accept His offer of forgiveness in Christ. Those who accept His offer are saved, those who refuse are lost. They choose to stay under God's wrath against sin and consign themselves to Hell.

This position avoids all the contradictions and problems of each side. No need to change the meaning of Greek words (saying "*kosmos*" means "the elect"); no need to accuse God of evil doing (saying He caused the fall); no need to deny the depravity of man; no need to deny man's ability to respond, with God's enabling to the call of salvation; no need to explain why God would, for no given reason and in contradiction to His loving nature, choose only a few and consign the rest of humanity to a Christless eternity. It is a position of balance, held in place by the tension of truth on the arms of the eternal scales of reality.

John Piper, in spite of his strong Calvinistic position, actually comes to this kind of balance in a talk on prayer. In this he shows his deep commitment to Scripture and his integrity as he speaks against his own Calvinistic position.

"It's simply staggering that God, would ordain--now get this--that the Ruler of the universe would ordain--now get this--that prayers CAUSE things. They do! That prayer causes things to happen that would not happen if you didn't pray. I wonder if there are any Calvinists out there squirming?

"Listen to this, when James 4:2 says, "You do not have, because you do not ask." That does not mean, "You would have anyway even if you didn't ask because I've got a plan!" The verse does not mean the opposite of what it says! It says, "You have not because you ask not." That means prayer causes things to happen that wouldn't happen if you didn't pray.

"This is why this is such a staggeringly glorious privilege. To be taken by the Sovereign God of the universe who works all things according to his infinite wisdom, and to fold it into his causality.

"This is breath-taking. If you do not avail yourself of the privilege of bringing to pass events in the universe, that would not take place if you didn't pray, you are acting like a colossal fool! Aren't you? I'm just thinking logically here.

"If you are offered the privilege of engaging with God in such a way that your request could bring into being things that would not otherwise come into being, Not to avail yourself of that privilege is folly of the highest or lowest order!

That's why we pray. He's beckoning us into our share, in the running of the universe. Do you not know that you will judge angels? Do you know who you are, child of God?"[20]

Martin Lloyd-Jones gives us a good summary:

...the great problem is this: if God does govern and control everything, then what is His relationship to sin? All

---

[20] https://www.youtube.com/watch?v=krzwmhDMvv8

I can do, in answer, is to lay down a number of propositions that are clearly taught in the Scriptures.

The first is that sinful acts are under divine control, and occur only by God's permission and according to His ultimate purpose. If you want proof of that you will find it in the case of Joseph and his brethren. 'So then, it was not you who sent me here, but God,' said Joseph (Gen. 45:8). God permitted their sinful act and controlled it.

You will find the same teaching about the death of our Lord as it is expounded by Peter on the Day of Pentecost (Acts 2).

The second is that God restrains and controls sin. In Psalm 76:10 we read, 'Surely the wrath of man shall praise you: the remainder of wrath shall you restrain.'

The third is that God overrules sin for good. Genesis 50:20 puts it like this: 'You intended to harm me, but God intended it for good to accomplish what is now being done, the saving of many lives.' God overruled the sin, and He did exactly the same in the case of the death of our Lord.

My last proposition is that God never causes sin, nor approves of it; He only permits, directs, restrains, limits and overrules it. People alone are responsible for their sin. The first chapter of James gives that particular teaching clearly.[21]

So, Let us willfully join Jesus in seeing His prayers answered, "My prayer is not for them [His disciples] alone. I pray also for those who will believe in me through their message, *that all of them may be one,* Father, just as you are in me and I am in you. May they also be in us *so that the world may believe* that you have sent me" (John 17:15,20-21).

Let us obey Paul's command to Timothy that is applicable here, "... charge them before God not to quarrel about words, which does no good, but only ruins the hearers" (2 Tim. 2:14). As we quibble over the meaning of words, like the elect, predestination, the cosmos and works, we harm believers and drive away inquirers.

---

[21] D. M. Lloyd-Jones, *God the Father, God the Son* (Wheaton, IL: Crossway Books: 1996), 150.

Let us join together to reach the world for Christ, to build up believers and to bring glory to God by having "the same attitude of mind toward each other that Christ Jesus had, *so that with one mind and one voice* you may glorify the God and Father of our Lord Jesus Christ. *Accept one another, then just as Christ accepted you, in order to bring praise to God*" (Romans 15:5-7; emphasis mine).

Part 2

My Personal Journey in Understanding Calvinism

Chapter 6
The Approach

As mentioned in the introduction, a Calvinist who heard me speak asked me to consider his theological position. I agreed to enter into dialogue with this fellow and for six months he and I had a spirited and intense email interaction on his views.

In order to settle my own thoughts on the matter, I continued to do research and then wrote a paper to help me think the whole matter through.

I was able to be quite objective in my research and conclusions because I was not comparing what I found with previous teaching I'd had. Instead I compared what I was learning with the Bible, the book I had studied for so many years. I was open to becoming a Calvinist if that was what the Scriptures proved to be the true conclusion.

As I have talked with Calvinists and read about their beliefs, it quickly became apparent that there is a diversity of positions. That is, there is a spectrum of beliefs among those who call themselves Calvinists or reformed believers.

It seems to me that many of them have been taught some about Calvinism and have superficially understood a number of its tenants but have not researched it for themselves. More importantly, it seems they have not thought through the implications of their beliefs, carrying them to their logical conclusions. These musings may be of help to them.

For those who are learning about or considering becoming a Calvinist, hopefully this will help them to clearly think through the issues and implications.

I would like 1 Corinthians 13 to be the measure of my treatise. God's love for all should be flowing through us to each other. We can have different theological positions on a number of items beyond the foundational Truths of Christianity but we must never forget that as true, born-again believers we have large areas of common agreement. We can and must "with one heart and mouth... glorify the God and father of our Lord Jesus Christ." (Rom. 15:5)

Within this unity there is room for healthy discussion and examination of the Word. We must speak the truth in love, or we do not love well. This examination of Calvinism is to be just such a discussion, like the one I had with the Calvinist who challenged me, and then with myself as I thought through the issues.

The conclusions I come to in this section are my own and for myself. *You, the reader, are free to disagree with me and come to your own conclusions.* Then we can graciously give each other the freedom to differ and move on together to reach the world for Christ.

In an effort to accurately portray Calvinistic beliefs, I have presented the points of Calvinism with the words of those who call themselves Calvinists, rather than give my own limited understanding.[1]

A Word About Calvin

John Calvin, from what I have read, was an intelligent, gifted and complex man with many sides. As a person and pastor, he had a heart for his people, was moved by suffering and did much to help those around him. He also had a heart for evangelism and trained others to go out and share. He was insightful, a hard worker and prolific writer. Judging from what I have read personally, some of his works, such as his commentaries, have many insightful and helpful passages.

His most famous work, "The Institutes" I have found, however, to be different, as were his actions that stemmed from following his theological system. Part of that may be the fact he wrote *the Institutes* during the first nine months after becoming a born again Christian. Not even the Apostle Paul did anything like that. He waited, needing at least three years of personal training from the Lord in the desert before he was mature enough to begin writing theological treatises.

I clearly and gladly acknowledge Calvin's good points, while I will not shrink back from seeing the aspects of his theology, life and work, which are of different quality.

---

[1] With the exception of quotes from Calvin's Institutes, which are taken from his own writings, all the quotes listed below were cited in the book, *What Love Is This?: Calvinism's Misrepresentation of God* by Dave Hunt (Sisters, Oregon: Loyal Publishing, 2002).

Chapter 7
Calvinism's View of God's Sovereignty

Calvinism is usually presented in its five points, but as I've studied them, it has become clear that the undergirding principle for all of them is Calvin's understanding of God's Sovereignty, so that is the place where we will start.

As with other points of Calvinism, it is easy to agree with the surface statement. Of course, God is sovereign. He created and rules the universe and is easily able to weave into His plan all that happens.

However, as one looks into it, there is much more to Calvin's belief than this. Calvinism has a specialized definition of God's sovereignty.

Here, in the words of Calvinists, is their confirmation of the importance of the Calvinistic understanding of the Sovereignty of God and their definition of it.

Talbot and Crampton write "The sovereignty of God is ...the most basic principle of Calvinism....the foundation upon which all is built."[2]

Boettner thinks the same, "The basic principle of Calvinism is the sovereignty of God." [3]

"The secret grandeur of Calvin's theology lies in his grasp of the biblical teaching of the sovereignty of God." says Singer[4]

Now let's look at what Calvin and his strong followers believe about the Sovereignty of God. As I quote the following authors, I would guess that there are some who call themselves moderate Calvinists who would not subscribe to this description of the Sovereignty of God, but I must take what Calvinists themselves have written as they honestly take their beliefs to their logical conclusions. I have emphasized important points in italics

Calvin in his Institutes wrote, "...God is the disposer and ruler of all things–that from the remotest eternity, according to

---

[2] Kenneth G Talbot and W. Gary Crampton, *Calvinism, Hyper-Calvinism and Arminianism* (Still Waters Revival Books, 1990), 14.

[3] Lorraine Boettner, *The Reformed Faith* (Presbyterian and Reformed Publishing Co., 1983), 2.

[4] C. Gregg Singer, *John Calvin: His Roots and Fruits* (A Press, 1989), 32.

his own wisdom, he decreed...that by his providence, not heaven and earth and inanimate creatures only, but also *the counsels and wills of men are so governed as to move exactly in the course which he has destined....*"

He continues, "In short, Augustine everywhere teaches...that there cannot be a greater absurdity than to hold that anything is done without the ordination of God *because it would happen at random.* For which reason, he *also excludes the contingency which depends on human will,* maintaining a little further on, in clearer terms, that *no cause must be sought for but the will of God...*"

"...the order, method, end and necessity of events, are, for the most part, hidden in the counsel of God, though it is certain that *they are produced by the will of God....*"[5]

Edwin H. Palmer makes it very clear what this sovereignty of God means: "All things that happen in the world at any time and in all history....*come to pass because God ordained them. Even sin*—the fall of the devil from heaven, the fall of Adam, and every evil thought, word and deed in all of history, including the worst sin of all, Judas' betrayal of Christ—*is included in the eternal decree of our holy God.*

He concludes with: "It is even biblical to say that *God has foreordained sin."*[6]

Boettner agrees with this conclusion: "Even *the fall of Adam,* and through him the fall of the race was not by chance or accident, but *was so ordained in the secret counsels of God."*[7]

Calvin says that God "foresees the things which are to happen, *simply because he has decreed that they are so to happen....*"[8] That is, God foreknows only because He has foreordained events.

Calvin admits this idea of God foreordaining sin is hard to accept: "The decree, I admit is dreadful; and yet it is impossible

[5] John Calvin, *Institutes of the Christian Religion,* trans. Henry Beveridge (Grand Rapids, MI: Wm. B. Erdmans Publishing Company, 1998 ed.), lxvi,6,8,9.

[6] Edwin H. Palmer, *The Five Points of Calvinism* (Baker Books, enlarged ed. 20th printing, 1999), 82, 97-100,116.

[7] Lorriane Boettner, *Reformed Doctrine of Predestination* (Presbyterian and Reformed Publishing Co., 1932), 234.

[8] Calvin, op. cit., III: xxiii, 6.

to deny that *God foreknew what the end of man was to be before he made him and foreknew because he had so ordained by his decree.*"[9]

Other Calvinists echo this theme. Grover Gunn states "The idea that God knows the future without having planned it and without controlling it is totally foreign to Scripture."[10] But he gives no references to back this up. That is most likely because there is no Scripture that confirms it.

Calvin adds another point to this picture: *"The first man fell because the Lord deemed it meet that he should....Man therefore falls, divine providence so ordaining, but he falls by his own fault*...the destruction consequent upon predestination is also most just."[11]

If I understand these statements correctly, here is what is being put forth:

1. God is totally in control of every event in the universe; nothing, not even the tiniest event, occurs without Him having, in their words, "decreed it" "caused it" "foreordained it." Otherwise it would "be random," that is out of God's control and therefore bad.

2. God is able to foreknow things only because he foreordained them.

3. This includes God foreordaining, decreeing (in Calvin's word, being the "cause" of) sin. God foreordained the fall, the murder of Able, the evil things done before the flood, and your every sinful thought, word and act. We have no choice but to sin because God decided before hand that we would do this.

4. No one and no thing can make a decision on their own; all is foreordained by God.

5. Even though God predestined us to sin, decreed our sinning, foreordained that we would do so, made us do

---

[9] Calvin, op. cit, III: xxii, 7.

[10] Grover Gunn, *The Doctrine of Grace* (Footstool Publications, 1987), 13.

[11] Calvin, op. cit. III: xxiii, 8.

it, gave us no possibility of not doing it, we are still held responsible for our sin.

These beliefs and conclusions are so far from my understanding of the biblical picture that one would think he is reading of a different religion.

As we have seen in previous chapters and shall see later, there are reams of Scripture that contradict this belief, which has more in common with Islam than what the Bible teaches.

Chapter 8
What Does the Bible Say About God's Character?

In looking at this theology of God's sovereignty, our reference needs to be Scripture. This means we must both carefully examine relevant verses and passages, and we must see how they fit into the overall scope of Scripture. This is a pattern we will follow in examining each point of Calvinist theology.

After we look at how this fits with the God of Scripture, we will look at some portions of Scripture Calvinists use to support their theology.

First and foremost, does the Calvanistic view of God's sovereignty line up with the character of God as presented in the Bible?

Looking at a few of His characteristics will make it clear where Scripture stands on the subject.

A. God is Holy

"Worship the Lord in the splendor of his holiness; tremble before him, all the earth." (Ps. 96:9) God here presents himself as holy—meaning pure, without sin, completely other than His creation—right from the beginning. As Jehovah He emphasizes this quality, "Who among the gods is like you, O Lord (Jehovah)? Who is like you—majestic in holiness..." (Ex. 15:1). In Isaiah 57:15 He declares, "For this is what the high and lofty One says–he who lives forever, whose name is holy: I live in a high and holy place...."

As we all know, this is then restated thousands of times in the Bible, ending with many proclamations in Revelation, such as "You are just in these judgments, you who are and who were, the Holy One...." (Rev. 16:5).

God is holy. He is pure. He is devoted to what is right. "In him is no sin" (1Jn. 3:5) and He hates sin: "You are not a God who takes pleasure in evil; with you the wicked cannot dwell. the arrogant cannot stand in your presence; you hate all who do wrong" (Ps. 5:4,5).

Being holy, He does not tempt men to sin. "...God can not be tempted with evil, nor does he tempt anyone; but each one is tempted when, *by his own evil desire*, he is dragged away and enticed." (Jas. 1:13,14).

On the contrary, He calls us to holiness: "But just as he who called you is holy, so be holy in all you do: for it is written, 'Be holy, because I am holy.'" (1Pe. 1:15,16). This if an oft repeated command, as seen in Leviticus. 11:44,45; 19:2; 20:7.

To think that a sinless God would make sure that men sinned, would make sure it was impossible for men NOT to sin, that He would foreordain the fall, the many evil acts and the suffering of the world—this is completely, absolutely the opposite of his Holiness.

On the contrary, He is the One who hates sin, who commands us not to sin, who commands us to be holy like him. He who hates sin would not, could not cause sin. He is clearly grieved when men do sin.

In seeking to grasp the implications of the God Calvin described, I thought of my friend's son who at age 12 was raped at gunpoint. Many years later he is still struggling with the damage done by that event. If Calvin were correct, we would have to say that God planned that rape of the boy, caused it to happen, foreordained it to happen. The God of the Bible, Praise His Name, is far from this! He is holy and hates sin rather than planning it.

"Let those who love the Lord hate evil..." (Ps. 97:10).

B. God is Righteous and Just

All through Scripture God presents Himself as being just, judging rightly: "Righteousness and justice are the foundation of your throne; love and faithfulness go before you" (Ps. 89:14).

A just God will judge justly. If, as the Calvinist believes, God causes man to sin, makes it impossible to NOT sin, then judges him for it, God is not just by His own definition or by any human definition. Such a concept is repugnant to even the totally ungodly. God, who is far more pure and just than we can imagine, is even further from such a concept.

C. God is Love

"O Israel, put your hope in the Lord, for with the Lord is unfailing love" (Ps. 130:7). "He is good and his love endures forever" (2Ch. 5:13).

Many of God's characteristics are expressed as adjectives; this one, however, is a noun: "Whoever does not love does not know God, because God is love" (1Jn. 4:9). It is the essence of God's heart and is repeated often throughout the Bible. In Psalm 136 alone the refrain "His love endures forever" is repeated 26 times! Because He is love, He cannot not love!

His love leads Him to do many things for His rebellious people, including sending His Son to be the Savior of the world: "This is how God showed his love among us: He sent his one and only Son into the world that we might live through him. This is love: not that we loved God, but that he loved us and sent his Son as an atoning sacrifice for our sins" (1Jn. 4:9,10).

He then calls us to imitate Him in this: "Dear friends, since God so loved us, we also ought to love one another" (1Jn. 4:11). "This is how we know what love is. Jesus Christ laid down his life for us and we ought to lay down our lives for our brothers" (1Jn. 3:16). "Greater love has no one than this: that he lay down his life for his friends" (Jn. 15:13). "But I tell you: Love your enemies and pray for those who persecute you, that you may be the sons of your Father in heaven" (Mt. 5:44,45).

To think that this God of love would foreordain people to sin—causing them to disobey Him, knowing that there would be terrible consequences—is totally contrary to how God presents His love in Scripture and how He wants us to follow His example.

Presbyterian theological professor and one-time Moderator of the General Assembly, Herrick Johnson understood this contradiction and wrote, "Across the Westminster Confession could justly be written: 'The Gospel for the elect only.' That Confession was written under the absolute dominion of one idea, the doctrine of predestination. It does not contain one of these three truths: God's love for a lost world; Christ's compassion for a lost world; and the gospel universal for a lost world."[12]

One researcher of Calvinism?" wrote: "There is no escaping the fact that in Calvin's entire *Institutes of the Christian Religion* that there is not one mention of God's love for the lost! Nor is that surprising in view of the fact that Calvin's God has no love for the lost but can only love the elect."[13]

The God who is love is very different from the one presented by the Calvinist.

D. God is Faithful

1. God is true to his character: "O Lord God Almighty, who is like you? You are mighty, O Lord, and your faithfulness surrounds you" (Psa. 89:8). God says that He is holy, that He hates sin, that He will punish it, so He will do this. God proclaims that He will always act in faithfulness to His revealed character; therefore we know that He will not do what is unholy, sinful or unjust. He cannot sin Himself; He cannot make man sin; he cannot judge unjustly.

Yet Calvin's system says that God is the willful and deliberate cause of evil; that He makes men sin (which is against the stated will of God as well as his character); that he judges men for doing what they are forced to do–they have no chance of *not* doing it.

2. God is faithful to His promises. Every promise He made is a voluntary restriction He placed on His sovereignty. When He said to David, "One of your own descendants I will place on your throne...for ever and ever," (Ps. 132:11), God restricted Himself to working with the descendants of David.

God, being much greater than the Calvinist thinks, is obviously able to contain and use the swirl of events caused by the real choices of men, and easily bring about his desired end. He's that big! "I know that the Lord is great, greater than all gods. The Lord does whatever pleases him...." (P.s 135:5,6a). If

---

[12] Quoted in Augustine H. Strong, *Systematic Theology* (Judson Press, 1907), 779.

[13] Dave Hunt, *What Love is This?: Calvinism's Misrepresentation of God* (Loyal Press, 2002), 151. Calvin, op. cit. II: xvi, 3-4; II:xvii,2-5.iii, 8.

it is His idea to limit His sovereignty in any way, who are we to object?

E. God is Sovereign.

"The Lord reigns; let the earth be glad; let the distant shores rejoice." (Ps. 97:1) He is in control, and we can rejoice because He is a good sovereign.

God is moving history to a conclusion, an inescapable fact. "He has set a day when He will judge the world with justice..." (Ac. 17:30). He has set limits for men's moral decisions while He is able to weave together the many decisions that mankind makes, whether of obedience or rebellion, and to use them to reach His goals. "The Lord will fulfill his purpose for me..." (Ps. 138:8). "The Lord does whatever pleases him..." (Ps. 135:6).

In spite of all the rebellion and disobedience of Israel, God brought salvation from their line at the right time. He used the rebellion of the Pharisees to accomplish His purpose. He used the prompting of Satan in Judas' heart to accomplish His purpose (note that Judas was prompted, not forced; he had to make a decision on his own and then he came under the control of Satan, who wants to be the kind of dictator Calvinists accuse God of being).

God calls for obedience, and promises to protect us by His sovereign power from evil: "Let those who love the Lord hate evil, for he guards the lives of his faithful ones and delivers them from the hand of the wicked" (Ps. 97:10).

Calvin himself believed God to be omnipotent but felt the need to defend Him, seeing man's being a free moral agent a threat to God: "If this frigid fiction [of man having a free will] is received, where will be the omnipotence of God, by which, according to his secret council on which everything depends, he rules over all?"[14] This is a false dilemma created by Calvin's system. God needs no man to protect His sovereignty!

Make no mistake, God is sovereign, and His giving mankind the privilege of being able to choose good or evil (see sections 2-6 below) has not threatened or lessened His

---

[14] Calvin, op. cit. III: xxiii, 6-7.

sovereignty in any way. This is *His* idea, not man's (!) and does not diminish his glory one iota. In fact, it highlights His greatness in being able to work with all that men do to still bring about His desired end.

On this point, even some Calvinists see the refutation in Scripture of Calvin's statement that God's sovereignty eliminates man's ability to make moral responsible decisions. D.A. Carson writes, "God's unconditional sovereignty and the responsibility of human beings are mutually compatible."[15]

I think of an illustration of God's sovereignty. A sheet of paper represents His sovereignty: everything that occurs there is under his power. Then He draws a circle for each person and within that sphere gives the person ability to make genuine moral and ethical decisions: to lie or tell the truth; to be mean or kind; to be diligent or lazy. In His sovereignty, He has given this ability, therefore it is not a threat to Him at all.

F. Does God want good or evil for mankind?

"The Lord delights in those who fear him, who put their hope in his unfailing love." (Psa.147:11). "The Lord is faithful to all his promises and loving toward all he has made. ... The Lord is righteous in all his ways and loving toward all he has made" (Ps. 147:13b,17).

It is His character to want His creatures to obey Him, to give them good, not to force them to sin. He is not pleased with those who sin, but at the same time does not want to see them die and go to hell. "I take no pleasure in the death of the wicked, but rather that they turn from their ways and live" (Ezk. 33:11a). He goes on to plead with the wicked: "Turn! Turn from your evil ways! Why will you die, o house of Israel?" (Ezk. 33:11b).

God's desire is stated clearly in the New Testament: "God our Saviour...will have *all men* to be saved..." (1Ti. 2:3b-4; emphasis mine) "He is patient with you, not wanting *anyone* to perish, but *everyone* to come to repentance" (2Pe. 3:9b; emphasis mine).

---

[15] D.A. Carson, *The Difficult Doctrine of the Love of God* (Crossway Books, 2000), 52.

Such a God would not force (i.e. predestine) all people into sin, judge them for what they could not avoid, then choose to save only a few while sending all the rest to Hell without any chance to be saved. He wants good, not evil for and from His creatures.

G. God is All-Knowing

God's foreknowledge is a common theme in Scripture: "Before a word is on my tongue you know it completely, O Lord" (Ps. 139:4). The God presented in the Bible is omniscient, omnipresent, omnipotent and infinite. I doubt that any Calvinist would dispute those descriptions of God.

If He is omniscient, then He knows all by definition, and there is no hint in Scripture that he is omniscient because He has foreordained every event, no matter how tiny. He is much greater than this: He is not bound by time, being outside of it—a fact spoken of by both Jehovah and Jesus: God said to Moses, say "'I am' has sent me..." (Ex. 3:14b). Jesus said, "Before Abraham was I am" (Jn. 8:58b). Other Scriptures also point to this: "One day is with the lord as a thousand years, and a thousand years as one day" (2Pe. 3:8). "...a thousand years in your sight are but as yesterday when it is past..." (Psa.90:4). "Great is our Lord and mighty in power; *his understanding has no limit*" (Ps. 147:5; emphasis mine). "Praise be to the name of God forever and ever. ... He reveals deep and hidden things; he knows what lies in darkness, and light dwells with him" (Dan. 2:20,22).

This idea of God needing to foreordain so He can foreknow is a philosophical construct stemming not from Scripture but from Augustine and the logic of Aristotle (everything must have a cause). It is a very limiting idea, making God much smaller than the All-knowing God of the Bible—one that will fit into a man's system limited by man's understanding.

A biblical statement would go more like this: God "knows all things possible, whether they be in the capability of God or of the creature ... imagination or enunciation ... all things that could have an existence ... those which are necessary and contingent, good and bad, universal and particular, future, present and past, excellent and vile. He knows the things substantial and accidental of every kind: actions and passions, the deliberations and counsels, and determinations and the entities of reason, whether complex or simple."[16]

The God who determines the number of the stars and calls them each by name (Ps. 147:4) is not reduced to foreordaining each event in order to know what will happen!

H. God is Balanced in His character

The Bible presents God as having many qualities, and these qualities as being balanced. Many times, when God is described, a number of His characteristics are mentioned together. For instance, in the Psalms it says, "...ascribe to the Lord *glory and strength*...worship the Lord in the splendor of His *holiness*" (Ps. 29:1,2; emphasis mine). "The Lord is *gracious and righteous; our God is full of compassion*" (Ps. 116:5; emphasis mine). "...for you are *good and ready to forgive and plenteous in mercy* to all who call on you" (Ps. 86:5; emphasis mine). "The Lord *watches over* all who love him, but all the wicked he will *destroy*" (Ps. 145:20; emphasis mine). There is no competition among these qualities; they are in harmony with each other.

A theology which does not follow the Bible in giving equal emphasis to all the qualities of God is, by definition, imbalanced. For instance, God is merciful, but his mercy does not negate his justice. Christ's death satisfied God's justice first and then His mercy could be freely given. Then "mercy triumphs over justice" (Jas. 2:13). Justice is satisfied and mercy flows.

God's love does not transgress His wisdom. His combination of compassion and wisdom lead him to wait sometimes before answering prayer, when love alone might act more quickly and spoil some of what could have been developed in the situation.

In Calvin's system, God's sovereignty seems to be viewed as God's MAJOR quality, overriding all others. This overemphasis seems to stem from a desire to protect God's sovereignty. Calvin's God must control everything, including

---

[16] Jacobus Ariminius, *The Works of James Ariminius,* trans. Marcus Dobs and William Nichols (Baker Book House, 1986), 2:120.

predestining sin, an obvious contradiction with the few traits we have looked at above. This reveals that Calvin's definition of God depends more on logic than on Scripture.

I. My conclusion for this section

The God presented in Calvinism does not line up with the way God presents Himself in Scripture. Calvin's theology fails this test. By over emphasizing the sovereignty of God, Calvin presents a scaled down version of the omnipotent Creator God of Scripture and makes a caricature of Him.

Chapter 9
Can Man Make Moral Decisions, Or Not?

Does the Calvinistic view of God's sovereignty line up with the way God set up the world? As He finished creating man, God said to him, "Rule over the fish of the sea and the birds of the air and over every living creature that moves on the ground" (Gen. 1:28). God's first command was for man to rule! He gave man responsibility and authority, a kingdom and subjects.

"The Lord God took the man and put him in the Garden of Eden to work it and care for it" (Gen. 2:15). Adam was not treated as one who could not make decisions. Quite the opposite, he was commanded to be in charge.

The Lord immediately had Adam exercise his authority: "The Lord God...brought them [all the beasts of the field and all the birds of the air] to the man to see what he would name them; and whatever the man called each creature, that was its name" (Gen 2:19). God watched this event with interest, seeing His creature join him in the creative process, bestowing names on what God had made. This is certainly not the picture of a God who had decided before hand what man would do and then caused the script to be played out down to its tiniest detail.

God's second command to Adam was one of restriction, "You are free to eat from any tree in the garden; but you must not eat from the tree of the knowledge of good and evil, for when you eat of it you will surely die" (Gen. 2:15). The fact God gave a negative command contains the proposition that man could disobey it--otherwise it would have been pointless. God forbade eating the fruit and promised punishment and loss for disobedience. For this to make sense, to be real, the man had to be able to choose for or against. But Calvin tells us Adam had no choice but to disobey.

Does this line up with the way God interacts with man?

There are many examples which show that God did not control every decision, every act, every thought of Adam and all who followed. I will pick just a few examples here.

A. The Flood

In Genesis 6 we read: "The Lord saw how great man's wickedness on the earth had become, and that every inclination of the thoughts of his heart was only evil all the time. The *Lord was grieved* that he had made man on the earth and his heart was filled with pain" (Gen. 6:5-6; emphasis mine).

This does not describe a God who controls every event, no matter how tiny. He had allowed men moral freedom, the ability to choose good or evil, and was not happy with what men were doing. He was pained, grieved, unhappy. What was happening was not what he wanted: men were not following God's will and it made God sad.

If God were the author of all this, as Calvin and his followers believe, this would be the situation:

1. The holy God would have forced men do evil things that displeased God, a contradictory thing for the holy, wise, all-knowing God to do.

2. God would have no reason to be sad; He, the perfect, wise, just God had foreordained that this evil would happen.

3. Although what men did was caused by God, God now would punish them. Remember the words of Augustine that Calvin quoted: "in clearer terms, that no cause must be sought for but the will of God...."

But none of these points match up with how it is described in Scripture. The story continues: "The Lord said, 'I will wipe mankind, whom I have created from the face of the earth...for I am grieved that I have made them.' But Noah found favor in the eyes of the Lord. Noah was a righteous man, blameless among the people of his time and he walked with God" (Gen 6:7-8).

Here God is sad over men in general, but pleased with Noah because Noah was righteous. If we look over into Hebrews, we find that Noah was righteous because of his faith: "by his faith he condemned the world and became heir of the righteousness that comes by faith" (Heb.11:7). It does not say that God made him be righteous, but that Noah responded to Him in faith. Other scripture tells us that faith comes by hearing the Word of God, so Noah was willing to listen to what God had to say.

Noah's faith, given through listening to the Word of God, brought him righteousness. He believed God and the result was being saved.

There is no hint of God making him believe, forcing him to obey, foreordaining his action; it says that Noah had faith and believed God, then received righteousness. God gave Noah instructions and Noah chose to obey them because of his faith.

Again, here is God interacting with man as if man were a moral creature, able to make real decisions. He commends man for obedience and punishes him for disobedience. This does not paint the picture of a God controlling every tiny decision. It is a God who is interacting with his creatures, allowing them to obey or disobey and then dealing with their acts.

There is a plethora of further examples that continue to illustrate how God Himself applies His own theology. I will list some briefly.

B. Moses

Moses tried to save his people in his own strength, including murdering a man; failing, he escaped to the wilderness where God prepared him for the right time to save Israel. In this God directed his steps, while allowing him to make his own mistakes.

When the time came for Moses to be the deliverer of his people, God appeared to Moses in the burning bush. He reasoned with Moses; Moses had excuses; God offered him help and support; Moses finally agrees. This is the process of convincing, bringing him to a willingness to cooperate, not a controlling of Moses' decision and actions, not a foreordaining of Moses' compliance. If it were foreordained, this interchange would be a charade and fully unnecessary, giving a false impression of how God actually controls every detail.

C. Psalm 107

The whole of Psalm 107 gives one example after another of how men were far from God and God created circumstances to help them see their need for a relationship with God. When they sought Him, He answered, rescued and guided them: "Then they cried out to the Lord in their trouble and he delivered them from their distress" (v.6). A relational approach, not a controlling one.

D. Paul

On one journey, Paul and his companions experienced God directing their steps. While in Galatia, they were "...kept by the Holy Spirit from preaching the word in the province of Asia" (Ac. 16:6). They obviously wanted to preach in Asia but were prevented. We are not told how, but God intervened and kept them from following through on their desire. Here we have the plans of man and the direction of God. But no sign of a "foreordained act."

The account goes on, "When they came to the border of Mysia, they tried to enter Bithynia, but the Spirit of Jesus would not allow them" (Ac. 16:7). Again, they had a plan, again God directed them to change it. This is the interaction of men and God in a genuine relationship; not the preplanned, foreordained script where men cannot decide.

That night, "Paul had a vision of a man of Macedonia standing and begging him, 'Come over to Macedonia and help us.' After Paul had seen the vision, we got ready at once to leave for Macedonia, concluding that God had called us to preach the gospel to them" (Ac. 16:9,10).

They correctly concluded that God was directing them; so they then made the decision to obey. There is no hint of a predestined act, of them being forced by God in some foreordained way. This was the intelligent interaction of God with his followers as they tried to do His will. God is sovereign in giving them direction, and they had to be willing to change plans and follow Him.

E. Peter

When God was ready for Peter to take the gospel to the Gentiles, He carefully taught Peter the principle that what God had cleansed Peter should accept. In Acts 10 Peter was given a vision three times of a sheet full of unclean animals. A voice commanded Peter to kill and eat, but his reply was "I have never eaten anything impure or unclean." Peter had his mind made up. But God was going to convince him to change it. The voice replied, "Do not call anything impure that God has made clean" (Ac. 10:9-16). God was preparing Peter for obedience, not a predestined action.

Shortly before this God had sent an angel to Cornelius instructing him to send for Peter (again, asking for a willing obedience, not a preprogrammed response). When Cornelius' messengers arrived, Peter was receiving his lesson, which the Spirit reinforced with these words, "Simon, three men are looking for you. So, get up and go downstairs. Do not hesitate to go with them, for I have sent them" (Ac. 10:19-20). Being prepared, and instructed, Peter obeyed.

Again, here is a very relational interaction between the Master and the servant: teaching, convincing, instruction, preparation, calling for a decision and obedience. No hint of foreordination or predestination in these events.

In the "rest of the story" we see even more clearly that God did not foreordain Peter's actions, controlling him like a robot. Paul tells how Peter later disobeyed this vision and direction, withdrawing from eating with Gentile believers when the Judaizers arrived on the scene.

This was just the opposite of what he had learned directly from God, and Paul opposed him to his face, "You are a Jew, yet you live like a Gentile and not like a Jew. How is it, then, that you force Gentiles to follow Jewish customs?" (Gal. 2:14). Peter strayed from the path, and God brought him back through Paul's rebuke. No predestination here; men making wrong decisions and then being corrected.

So, we see that these examples speak against the Calvinistic idea of a sovereign God who must control every event to protect His sovereignty.

Chapter 10
Revealing Questions

1. Does the Calvinist concept of God's "total control sovereignty" line up with the many guidelines God has given and the way people have disobeyed them?

We will look at a few examples to come to a conclusion.

A. "But the Pharisees and experts in the law *rejected God's purpose for themselves*, because they had not been baptized by John" (Lk. 7:30). God had a purpose for these men, but they were able to refuse it. This Scripture shows clearly that men are able to reject what God wanted for them. If He were the "total control-God" of Calvin and many of his followers quoted at the beginning of chapter 9, this would not be possible.

B. Nehemiah, in his prayer in chapter 9 said, "You told them to go in and take possession of the land you had sworn with uplifted hand to give them. But they, our forefathers, became arrogant and stiff-necked, *and did not obey your commands. They refused to listen* and failed to remember the miracles you performed among them. They became stiff-necked and *in their rebellion* appointed a leader in order to return to their slavery" (Neh. 9:15b-17a; emphasis mine). These men were able to reject the direct commands of God.

C. In an opposite example, in Psalm 145:18 we are told, "The Lord is near to all who call on him, *to all who call on him in truth*." (emphasis mine) Those who choose to call on Him will be answered and helped, those who don't won't.

D. In 2 Thessalonians 2:10 we read, "They perish because *they refuse to love the truth* and so be saved." (emphasis mine) This is contrary to God's stated desire in 1 Timothy 2:4 "...that all men be saved...." People can choose against what God wants.

E. God gives us directives like this one: "For God did not call us to be impure but to live a holy life. Therefore, *he who rejects this instruction does not reject man but God* who gives you his Holy Spirit" (1Th. 4:7,8; emphasis mine). This passage assumes that men can reject God and His command, "...*he who rejects....*"

We all know people who say they are believers and violate this command for holiness, reject it blatantly, grossly, regularly, rejecting God and His commands. In fact, if we are honest about it, every one of us disobeys this and similar commands in daily life, in thought, if not in action. We are able to choose against what God wants.

F. In addition, there is a real and debilitating paradox created by the Calvinist's view (in contrast to many seeming paradoxes in the Bible). Calvin taught that people's sinning was foreordained by God, making it the will of God for them to sin; He decreed and caused it. This means it was God's will for them to reject God's stated will in Scripture.

This is both a paradox and an oxymoron and goes contrary to everything God says He wants: "Be ye holy as I am holy." Either God is a liar (He doesn't really want us to be holy) or the Calvinist view of God is wrong, or there is a third way.

Some Calvinists are aware of this problem. Palmer writes, "Although sin and unbelief are contrary to what God commands (perceptive will), God has included them in His sovereign decree (ordained them, caused them to certainly come to pass)....How is it that a holy God, who hates sin, not only passively permits sin but also certainly and efficaciously decrees that sin shall be? Our infinite God presents us with some astounding truths...."[17]

This is more than astounding: it is horrible, illogical, truly paradoxical, unbiblical doctrine, an insult to the character of God and in the end, heresy!

---

[17] Palmer, op. cit. 97-100, 116

2. Does this line up with God's invitation for people to come to Him and obey Him?

I have not counted how many times in the Bible God calls out to sinners to come to Him, but it is certainly hundreds of times. "Come unto me all you who are weary and heavy laden and I will give you rest." "I stretched out my arms to you, but you would not." "O Jerusalem, Jerusalem, you who killed the prophets and stoned them who were sent to you, how often would I have gathered your children together...and ye would not" (Mt. 23:37). "Return faithless people; I will cure you of backsliding" (Jer. 3:22). "For God so loved the world that he gave his only begotten son that whoever believes in him should not perish but have eternal life" (Jn. 3:16).

Either these are real expressions of God's desire and invitation for people to come to Him through His provision of a way through Christ—or they are a sham.

If God controls every tiny event, including who can come to Him and who can't, then these invitations are not real. This will become evident when we look at Calvinism's views on the depravity of man and unconditional election. In Calvin's view, the elect will come, willing or not; the non-elect can't come no matter what. However, the biblical record shows a different picture: a compassionate God who does really call out to all people, and provides the help they need to respond.

3. Does this line up with the biblical concept of Love? Can love be programmed?

God in Scripture woos people: He calls, encourages, gives light, instructs, reveals and gives insight. But nowhere does He force people to love Him, for the very definition of love is contrary to this: love is given, not forced.

If God determines ahead of time that a person will love him, and the person has no choice but must do it, this is forced to "love," which by definition is not love, but being programed.

Even unbelievers understand this. I heard that in the movie "Bruce Almighty" Bruce asks, "How can I force someone with free will to love me?" God answers, "You can't!" This quote, of course is no authority, it simply reveals the illogicity of the idea of forcing people to love.

Forced, predestinated love is another oxymoron. For it to be real love there must be the possibility to choose not to love. The God of the Bible knows that we can respond or reject His offer of love because that is the way He made us. That is part of being made in His image.

4. Is God a Dictator?

Calvinists believe that if men are able to make choices independent from the control of God, God's sovereignty would be compromised. This paints the picture of a very small-minded ruler whose sovereignty must be protected. King Saul was such a ruler, wanting to control everything, not able to see the loyalty of David, seeing him instead as competition.

Fortunately, God is different than that: "Praise be to the Lord, to God our Savior, who daily bears our burdens. Our God is a God who saves; from the Sovereign Lord comes escape from death" (Psa. 68:19). He is a sovereign who is gracious and loving rather than despotically controlling.

It takes a much bigger God, the God of the Bible, to give men the ability to choose within certain limits—as God gave Adam in the garden, Jonah in the ship, Moses at the burning bush, and David after seeing Bathsheba—-and then to weave all their choices into the plan He will ultimately bring to pass.

Think of it on a human level: men like Hitler, Stalin, Saddam Hussein and the ruler of North Korea had to control everything in their kingdoms to maintain their sovereignty. It takes a much greater man to rule his domain with grace, giving definite boundaries, but allowing his subjects to be freely creative within those boundaries. Churchill and Abraham Lincoln are examples of such a leader.

One type of leader produces a cold, oppressive environment with people woodenly doing what they are commanded (I have personally observed this visiting in communist countries in the 1980s); the other produces a growing, positive, creative environment where people can choose to blossom and add to the good of all.

Paul's admonition to the Ephesians shows which kind of King our God is: "I urge you to live in a manner worthy of your calling. That you be completely humble and gentle. Be patient, bearing with one another in love. Doing all you can to keep the unity of the Spirit in the bond of peace."

God is calling us to cooperate with the up building of the Body of Christ. He has given us a real part in this. God has given us the ability to choose to obey Him, or to refuse to obey Him. If there were no such choice, these commands would be utterly senseless and useless.

5. Does this line up with what the Bible says on who is responsible for evil?

God set the scene right from the beginning with these words "Rule over" the earth and "you must not eat from the tree of knowledge..." (Gen. 1:28; 2:17). He made man a moral creature: real responsibility, real limits, real consequences.

Adam chose to sin. There is no hint that God forced him to do this. And God immediately held each party involved responsible: Satan, Adam and Eve each were faced with their sin; each had consequences to bear.

In contrast, the Calvinist says that God foreordained that men would sin, but then holds them responsible for what they could not avoid. Think of this on a human level: a father forces his 5-year-old daughter to be involved in prostitution. When caught, who will be held responsible? Certainly, the father will not be guiltless. Augustine and Calvin both call God the "cause of all," including the fall. That belief, by any standard, makes God the source of evil.

Wonderfully, God is not the source of evil as the Calvinist system dictates. God is the solution to evil. Therefore we can have hope!

6. Was Calvin himself able to live within his own view of God's Sovereignty?

Believing that God has foreordained every great act as well as every trivial act every human being will ever commit, may make life easier in some ways ("God made me do it!").

Knowing that the embarrassing thing I just did was planned without my consent or knowledge and that I had no choice but to do it, should make it easier to accept. It may make it easier to forgive myself, let go and move on to the next act that I will be forced to be involved in.

However, a more realistic outlook of following this doctrine of God's total-control sovereignty, is that one either becomes very fatalistic and irresponsible, or one has to ignore the daily implications of such a belief. Calvin seemed to take this second course. A significant incident illustrates this.

During Calvin's time in Geneva, a group of early reformists called the Waldensians experienced a brutal attack from the Catholic rulers in their area. Calvin wrote to a friend on May 4, 1545 about this atrocity, saying he received a report that "...several villages have been consumed by fire, that most of the old men have been burned to death, that some had been put to the sword, others having been carried off to abide their doom; and such was the savage cruelty of these persecutors, that neither young girls, nor pregnant women, nor infants were spared. So great is the atrocious cruelty of this proceeding, that I grew bewildered when I reflect upon it. How, then shall I express it in words?"[18]

Humanly speaking, Calvin showed compassion, horror and dismay– appropriate reactions to such a terrible happening. However, when we remember his own words and his quote from Augustine, his response does not follow his theology. "...God is the disposer and ruler of all things... the counsels and wills of men are so governed as to move exactly in the course which he has destined...." He continues, "In short, Augustine everywhere teaches...that no cause must be sought for but the will of God..."[19]

He says that it is not human will that is the cause, but it is God Himself. Ergo Calvin should just accept this atrocity as planned and executed by God and move on. But he cannot respond this way, for it is against his own compassion and certainly against everything God shows Himself to be. The irrationality of his theology is seen in the mirror of everyday life. We saw this in the life of one Calvinistic friend who is often aggravated with the way people drive. I asked him, "if it is

---

[18] John Calvin, *Letters of John Calvin, Volume 1*, p. 434, quoted in Reform and Revival, Vol 10, Number 4, Fall 2001, 51.

[19] John Calvin *Institutes* op. cit. I: xvi, 6,8,9.

predestined, why get upset?" He did not like that question, as it exposed the illocgicity of his response to an everyday situation.

Chapter 11
Some passages Calvinists use

As a second major area, we will look at some of the favorite passages Calvinists use to prove their position. In evaluating how these passages might support the Calvinistic perspective, we will look at these verses in context, both immediate and in the whole scope of Scripture.

A. Psalm 37:23

"The steps of a man are established by the Lord; and He delights in his way." This is said to prove that each action of a man is predetermined by God. Is this what it actually says?

Psalm 37 is written by David as advice to believers who face opposition from the wicked ("Fret not yourself because of evil doers..."). David gives a list of comparison and contrast between the wicked and the righteous. For example, "The wicked borrows and does not pay back, but the righteous is gracious and gives. For those blessed by Him will inherit the land; but those cursed by Him will be cut off."

These are the two verses that precede verse 23, which in the NASB translates, "The steps of a man are established by the Lord; and He delights in his way." and the next verse continues, "When he falls, he shall not be hurled headlong; because the Lord is the One who holds his hand."

The whole context speaks of how God helps and blesses those who obey and punishes those who don't: "Rest in the Lord and wait patiently for Him; do not fret because of him who prospers in his way. ... for evil doers will be cut off but those who wait for the Lord, they will inherit the land" (37:7-9).

Verse 23, taken in this context does not speak of God's total control of every single detail of a righteous man's life. It speaks of how God helps and guides a man.

A look at the NIV brings this out even more clearly: "If the Lord delights in a man's way, he makes his steps firm; though he stumble he will not fall, for the Lord upholds him with his hand."

It is clearly an interaction, a partnership between man and God. The Lord helps and guides those who are seeking to walk in His way. There is no hint of a total control sovereignty here where every decision, no matter how tiny, is made by God beforehand; in fact it speaks of the opposite, with men choosing to obey and God encouraging them along.

B. Proverbs 16:9

"In his mind a man plans his course, but the Lord determines his steps" (NIV), or "The mind of man plans his way. But the Lord directs his steps" (NASB). Taken by itself, it is possible to infer from this verse that God does predestine, cause, foreordain every decision of a man, overriding what the man plans.

Some preceding verses support this viewpoint ("The Lord works out everything for his own ends—even the wicked for a day of disaster" (Pr. 16:4), making it sound like the Lord is working on His own without any part played by men.

On the other hand, some verses in the context do not support this idea: "When a man's ways are pleasing to the Lord, he makes even his enemies to be at peace with him" (Pr. 16:7) and "Through love and faithfulness sin is atoned for; through the fear of the Lord a man avoids evil," Pr. 16:6). Here man does what is right and the Lord responds by protecting him and keeping him from doing evil. So, from the context we can conclude that a "total control" interpretation is only partially supported.

Let's look to see how this verse fits into the broader context of Scripture and how God applies this verse Himself. The book of Jonah gives us a clear picture.

God commanded Jonah to go and preach in Nineveh. As you probably know, this city was a powerful enemy of Israel, and Jonah did not want to go preach there; he preferred the destruction of the enemy. Jonah's response was that he "ran away from the Lord and headed for Tarshish" (Jnh. 1:3). God did not stop him from running away; he allowed Jonah to disobey, to act against the stated will of God.

The Lord, however, set limits on how much Jonah would be allowed to rebel; that is, He "directed his steps." God's response to Jonah's decision was to send a storm to catch the ship Jonah had boarded. When the sailors cast lots to find out who had caused the problem, God directed and Jonah was chosen. He knew what had to be done: the sailors had to throw him overboard. And then came the big fish.

Here we see God's biblical sovereignty: he sent the storm, caused the lot to fall to Jonah, informed Jonah of what was to be done and caused the fish to be there and to swallow Jonah. This is God controlling the events and giving direction to Jonah's life.

While in the fish Jonah wrestled with his situation and, in the end, came to surrender: "When my life was ebbing away, I remembered you, Lord. ... What I have vowed I will make good" (Jnh. 2:7,9b). And when Jonah willingly surrendered, God sovereignly caused the fish to vomit Jonah out on dry land.

Note that God interacted with the fish and Jonah in two very different ways: God just commanded the fish and it obeyed; Jonah He brought to willing surrender. He treated Jonah as one who could choose, but gave him only so much room to rebel. God obviously sets definite limits on how much ability people have to choose; God controls the overall flow of events while giving humans ability to choose to obey or not within set limits.

The story goes on in the same fashion. Jonah preaches; the people repent. Because the people repent, God relents. Here God does not control the people like puppets, he has sent them a message, they received, feared and repented. Therefore, God decides not to destroy them. Real decisions brought real change in their future.

God is not done, however. Although Jonah as a preacher is very successful, he is unhappy because he wanted the city destroyed. He knows God's character well, "I knew that you are a gracious and compassionate God, slow to anger and abounding in love, a God who relents from sending calamity" (Jnh. 3:2). He knows that God responds to repentance; that He does not control every tiny action of man, but is grieved by sin and happy with repentance.

God continues to work with Jonah, not by controlling him, but by reasoning with him. He uses the vine as an object lesson (appealing to Jonah's heart) and an argument (appealing to his mind): "You have been concerned about this vine...but Nineveh has more than 120,000 people...should I not be concerned about that great city?" (Jnh. 4:10,11).

Here is the heart of God, full of compassion for those who are living in disobedience; He wants to save them and sends His messenger to warn and bring them to repentance.

If God were the one Calvinists envision, all His interaction with Jonah would be unnecessary; God would just decide and execute, no need to reason, teach, bring to surrender. He would treat people as he treated the fish. Instead God treats people as individuals who can choose to obey or not. God then weaves their obedience and disobedience into the fabric of his final and inescapable plan, just as He did with Jonah's disobedience and stubbornness. Either this is a charade or it is the real world God has created. The Bible certainly points to the second.

Chapter 12
Romans 9

There are definite verses in this chapter which sound like the Calvinistic view of a totally controlling God.

In verses 11-24 we read the following:

Yet, before the twins were born or had done anything good or bad—in order that God's purpose in election might stand: not by works but by him who calls–she was told, "The older will serve the younger." Just as it is written, "Jacob I loved, but Esau I hated."

What then shall we say? Is God unjust? Not at all! For he says to Moses, 'I will have mercy on whom I have mercy, and I will have compassion on whom I have compassion. It does not, therefore, depend on man's desire or effort, but on God's mercy. For the Scripture says to Pharaoh: "I raised you up for this very purpose, that I might display my power in you and that my name might be proclaimed in all the earth." Therefore God has mercy on whom he wants to have mercy, and he hardens whom he wants to harden.

One of you will say to me, 'Then why does God still blame us? For who resists his will?' But who are you, O man, to talk back to God? 'Shall what is formed say to him who formed it, "why did you make me like this?" Does not the potter have the right to make out of the same lump of clay some pottery for noble purposes and some for common use?

What if God, choosing to show his wrath and make his power known, bore with great patience the objects of his wrath–prepared for destruction? What if he did this to make the riches of his glory known to the objects of his mercy, whom he prepared in advance for glory–even us whom he also called, not only from the Jews but also from the Gentiles?

As with any good approach to Scripture, it is important to see the whole context, to understand what is going on here, and to make sure our understanding rises out of Scripture instead of forcing our understanding or theology onto Scripture.

In the larger context, Paul is writing to the Romans, explaining the overall plan of salvation that God has laid out over history and consummated in Christ's death and resurrection. The major theme is the one that struck Luther's eye and heart: "The just shall live by faith."

Paul emphasizes over and over in the preceding chapters that it is faith, not works, through which a person is saved. He particularly emphasizes to the Jews that it is not keeping the law that saves a man: "a man is a Jew if he is one inwardly; and circumcision is circumcision of the heart, by the Spirit, not by the written code" (Rom. 2:29).

Chapter 8 is the one of triumph, the victory of Christ over the weakness of the flesh, and how we share in that victory.

As he moves into Chapter 9, Paul focuses on the Jews and his desire to see them saved. His emphasis here is that God chooses the way of salvation, and it is not what the Jews have thought. "Yet, before the twins were born or had done anything good or bad—in order that God's purpose in election might stand: not by works but by him who calls...." (Rom. 9:11). God's purpose in election is to de-emphasize (eliminate) works as the means of salvation and to point to the salvation He provides apart from anything man can provide.

One twin was to be saved, one condemned, but not according to their works. According to what then? The answer to that is the whole theme of Romans: We are saved by *faith*. It is important to note that God calls many to belief, with the Holy Spirit convicting the whole world of sin, righteousness and justice, not just the elect (Mt. 22:14). So, one was saved by faith, demonstrated by his obedience, the other condemned by lack of faith, demonstrated by his disobedience.

It continues on to say, "...she was told, 'The older will serve the younger.' Just as it is written 'Jacob I loved, but Esau I hated'" (Rom. 9:12-13).

Since God knew what kind of men Jacob and Esau would be, He could easily make this statement. Scripture tells us that Esau placed no value on spiritual things: "See that no one is ... godless like Esau, who for a single meal sold his inheritance rights as the oldest son. Afterward, as you know, when he wanted to inherit this blessing, he was rejected. He could bring about no change of mind, though he sought the blessing with tears" (Heb 12:16,17). Esau's values were totally of this world (godless), and he could not bring himself to repent of this, so was rejected. He exercised no faith.

Jacob started out no better, was a deceiver, set his heart on the wrong things, but in the end submitted after God worked long and patiently to bring him to a place of surrender. "By faith Jacob, when he was dying, ... worshiped as he leaned on the top of his staff" (Heb. 11:21). Jacob was saved by faith.

This verse is a statement that God knows what a person will be, whether he will respond in faith to the gospel or not. And emphasizes that it is not a person's works but his faith that saves him; all the glory goes to God. It does not say that God decreed one to believe and the other not to.

The emphasis continues: God is the source of salvation and He decides to whom it will be given: "What then shall we say? Is God unjust? Not at all! For he says to Moses, 'I will have mercy on whom I have mercy, and I will have compassion on whom I have compassion.' It does not, therefore, depend on man's desire or effort, but on God's mercy." (Rom 9:14-16)

Man cannot do anything to earn God's bestowal of compassion and mercy; conversely, it depends on God's will. And upon whom does God have mercy? "You are forgiving and good, O Lord, abounding in love to *all who call to you*" (Ps 86:5). "Come to me, *all you* who are weary and burdened, and I will give you rest" (Mt. 11:28).

John says to all his readers, "These are written that *you* may believe that Jesus is the Christ, the Son of God and that by believing you may have life in his name" (Jn. 20:31).

"For *God so loved the world* [the *kosmos*, all of creation, not just the elect] that he gave his only son that *whosoever* believes in him shall not perish but have everlasting life" (Jn. 3:16; emphasis mine).The door is open to all because God opened it, totally apart from what man can do.

Then Paul gives a specific example of how God controls people and events to bring about His desired end while at the same time leaving them moral, responsible creatures: "For the Scripture says to Pharaoh: 'I raised you up for the very purpose, that I might display my power in you and that my name might be proclaimed in all the earth.'" (Rom 9:17)

If we look at the story of Moses and Pharaoh in Exodus 4 – 14, an interesting point comes out. The first six times Pharaoh's heart is hardened, it is not hardened by God, but by Pharaoh himself: after the plague of frogs, "When Pharaoh saw that there was relief, he hardened his heart and would not listen, just as the Lord had said" (Ex. 8:15). After the plague of gnats, "But Pharaoh's heart was hard and he would not listen, just as the Lord had said" (Ex. 8:19).

Note also, that although it is not the Lord's doing, He predicted that Pharaoh would harden his heart, for God knows the future whether he foreordains an event or not: "...just as the Lord had said."

The seventh time, after the plague of boils, it says, "But the Lord hardened Pharaoh's heart..." (Ex. 9:12). And this was true for the next three times also. God knew what kind of man Pharaoh was, that he would harden his heart to decide against God, but He still gave him six opportunities to submit to God's plan; after that God stepped in and hardened his heart.

Here again is the interaction between God and man, which gives each a part, foreknowledge without foreordaining. Then after a point is reached, God cements the man into his own chosen course.

The interesting thing is that Pharaoh's final recorded decision is described as his own, not God's: "Pharaoh and his officials changed their minds...." (Ex. 14:5b) and decided to pursue the Israelites, bringing about their own demise. Even at that late stage God stepped back and let them go on with their own decisions.

The conclusion? "Therefore God has mercy on whom he wants to have mercy, and he hardens whom he wants to harden" (Rom. 9:18). But it is not an arbitrary decision on His part; He offers mercy to all, including Pharaoh, but after the person refuses to heed a number of warnings, God gives them no more opportunity.

Then come the very "Calvinistic verses". "One of you will say to me, 'Then why does God still blame us? For who resists his will?' But who are you, O man, to talk back to God? Shall what is formed say to him who formed it, 'Why did you make me like this?' Does not the potter have the right to make out of the same lump of clay some pottery for noble purposes and some for common use?" (Rom. 9:20,21).

Paul here again points to God's right to decide how the world will go—but in the context of a God who gives chances to believe before hardening one's heart. When God decides enough opportunity has been given, that a man has "crossed the limit," He can justly harden the heart and close the door.

It is important to note here that Paul uses this same imagery in another place with the clear statement that a vessel made for common use can become one for noble purposes: "In a large house there are many articles...some are for noble purposes and some for ignoble. If a man cleanses himself from the latter, he will be an instrument for noble purposes, made holy, useful to the master and prepared to do any good work" (2Ti. 2:20,21).

"What if God, choosing to show his wrath and make his power known, bore with great patience the objects of his wrath–prepared for destruction?" (Rom. 9:22). It is important to note that according to Paul in Ephesians 2, we were all objects of God's wrath until we came to Him by faith. This same possibility of escaping God's wrath, according to God's oft-repeated invitation, is open to all ("For God did not send his Son into the world to condemn the world, but to save the world through him. *Whoever* believes in him is not condemned;" Jn. 3:17,18)

Second, we also know that some of the objects of God's wrath are Satan and his fallen angel followers, and that Hell, in fact, was prepared for primarily for them, not for us.

Third, part of the reason for God's patience is His giving further opportunity for faith and repentance: "He is patient with you, *not wanting anyone to perish, but everyone to come to repentance"* (2Pe. 3:9b; emphasis mine).

Paul continues: "What if he did this to make the riches of his glory known to the objects of his mercy, whom he prepared in advance for glory–even us whom he also called, not only from the Jews but also from the Gentiles?" (Rom. 9:22-24). Here is the purpose of his patience repeated, that more may come to Christ so his glory may be more widely known through his mercy flowing to more who have believed.

Now as we move into chapter 10 of Romans, Paul summarizes his argument, emphasizing God's right to decide who will be saved (those who believe) and how they will be saved (by faith), to man's responsibility in the matter. "...the Israelites...did not know the righteousness that comes from God and sought to establish their own, they did not submit to God's righteousness" (Rom. 10:2,3).

Then Paul goes on with a very "Arminian" passage: "...the righteousness that is by faith says: ... 'The word is near you; it is in your mouth and in your heart,' that is, the word of faith we are proclaiming: That if you confess with your mouth, 'Jesus is Lord,' and believe in your heart that God raised him from the dead, you will be saved. For it is with your heart that you believe and are justified, and it is with your mouth that you confess and are saved" (Rom. 10:8-10).

Here we are called upon to believe, to respond to the message, to "take advantage" of the Lord's extended mercy, proffered to all: "As the Scripture says, 'Anyone who puts trust in him will never be put to shame'" (Rom. 10:11; Isa. 28:16).

Yes, salvation is from God, 100%. God decides who will have mercy; that is, He extends it to all. God decides who will be saved, that is, all who respond to the gospel, and all can respond because of the several things God does to make it possible. These will be discussed later on.

Chapter 13
Romans 8:29-30

*For those God foreknew he also predestined to be
conformed to the likeness of his Son, that he might be the
firstborn among many brothers. And those he predestined,
he also called; those he called he also justified; those he
justified, he also glorified.*

The focus of discussion here is on the word "foreknew."
The Calvinists insist that this means he foreordained. John Piper
puts it this way: "The plain point of this passage is that God is
working infallibly to save his people, from foreknowing in
eternity past to glorifying in eternity future. None is lost at any
stage of redemption along the way. Nevertheless, this text is
often used to argue against unconditional election on the basis
of verse 29 which says, 'Those whom he foreknew he also
predestined.' Some say that people are not chosen
unconditionally; rather they are chosen on the basis of their
faith which they produce by their own powers of self
determination. God sees this self-determining choice by his
divine foreknowledge and responds by choosing and
predestining the believer to Christlikeness and glory."[20]

Piper here is nearly right in his characterization of the non-
Calvinistic view – but misses the most important point: no one
can "produce [faith] by their own powers of self determination."
That is an Arminian view. Biblically, faith clearly "comes by
hearing and hearing by the Word of God" (Rom. 10:17). Piper
has set up a straw man, which is easily knocked down.

Piper gives two reasons for establishing that God's
unconditional election is proven here. First is that all who are
called in this passage believe, so this is not the general call
extended to all, but a particular call. This I can agree with, but
Piper goes further to say, "...the called in this view must be the
act of God whereby he calls faith into being. And since it

---

[20] John Piper, *The Pleasures of God* (Multnomah Press, 1991), 139,140.

necessarily results in justification, it must be effectual or irresistible."[21]

That fits nicely with Piper's theology, but is an incorrect conclusion for the passage, which says nothing of the kind. It only says that those whom he calls he justifies, not that it is irresistible. Note that those whom he calls here are ones he knew beforehand would decide to believe.

The second argument concerns the word "foreknew" and has two parts. He first argues, "When Paul says in verse 29, 'Those whom he foreknew he also predestined,' he can't mean...that God knows in advance who will use their power of self-determination to come to faith...because we have seen from verse 30 that people do not come to faith on their own. They are called effectually. ...so the divine call guarantees faith."[22]

Much is being read into the passage here. Piper assumes that God "causes faith." He rejects the Bible's stance that it is the response of a man to the gospel (faith comes by hearing) and to the working of the Holy Spirit (convicting of sin, righteousness and judgment). Instead he declares that God's calling in verse 30 is "the act of God whereby he calls faith into being....and since it necessarily results in justification, it must be effectual or irresistible."[23] So a person has no choice to believe; he must, he is forced to believe. As we have seen elsewhere, this does not line up with scripture. God calls all, desires all to come, but only some come.

His second argument is based on his first argument and deals with the meaning of "foreknew." Piper writes, "So the foreknowledge of Romans 8:29 is not the mere awareness of something that will happen in the future apart from God's effective [irresistible] grace. Rather it is the kind of knowledge referred to in OT texts like Genesis 18:19 'I have chosen [Heb. *yada*'; literally: known] Abraham so that he may charge his children to... keep the way of the Lord.'...Such foreknowledge is virtually the same as election: 'Those whom he foreknew (that is chose) he predestined....'"[24]

---

[21] Piper, op. cit., 140.

[22] Piper, op. cit., 141.

[23] Piper, op. cit., 141.

[24] Piper, op. cit., 141.

In actuality, this word means exactly what it says, God knew ahead of time. It does not contain any indication of choosing or electing or predestinating in the word itself.

First of all, the word "foreknow" in Romans 8:29 and "chosen" 1 Peter 1:2 are both used in conjunction with the word predestine or chosen ("whom he foreknew he also predestined" and "chosen according to the foreknowledge of God"). If "foreknow" means to elect, to foreordain, to predestinate, then it is redundant giving us this reading: "whom he predestined he predestined" and "chosen according to the choosing of God." This, of course, does not make sense.

Second, Dr. C Gordon Olsen points out that in linking foreknow with the OT Hebrew word *yada'*, claiming it has the meaning of chosen, "Calvinists claim this pregnant meaning in only five out of 944 times yada' is used in the Old Testament, when overwhelmingly it has a meaning directly related to 'to know.' The standard Hebrew lexicon, the BDB version of Genesis, does not list any such pregnant meaning."[25]

Olsen also points out that, "We must always give preference to the primary meaning of a word in every context unless the context demands a secondary or tertiary meaning which has been established in other contexts as well."[26]

Concerning the word *proginoskein* (verb) and *prognosis* (noun) Dr. Olsen says, "There is no pregnant connotation of elective choice hinted at in the Septuagint, in classical Greek usage, in the Koine Greek as found in the papyrii and inscriptions, in Philo or Josephus, nor in the church fathers before Augustine. The verb simply means, 'to know beforehand, foreknow' and the noun, 'foreknowledge' or 'prescience.'"[27]

So to take the Scripture for what it says, seems to be the most honest approach. Those whom God foreknew (knew ahead of time) he predestined. No need for all the mental gymnastics to make it fit the Calvinistic viewpoint.

---

[25] Dr. C. Gordon Olsen, *Beyond Calvinism and Arminianism, an Inductive, Mediate Theology of Salvation* (Global Gospel Publishers, 2002), 155

[26] Olsen, op. cit., 156.

[27] Olsen, op. cit., 157

Chapter 14
Serious Biblical Problems in this View

The Calvinistic view of God's sovereignty creates a number of difficult problems for the serious Bible student, as listed below.

1. *God becomes the cause of evil.*
    a. God states His will, then causes men to transgress it.
    b. It is the will of God that His will be transgressed!
    c. It is the will of God that horrible acts are committed.
2. *People are punished for acts they are forced to commit* by the judge.
3. *Love is impossible*—true love cannot be forced or programed.
4. *Prayer is pointless*—what is predestined will happen anyway.
5. *Evangelism is pointless*—the elect will come no matter what.

If the Calvinistic view that God has predestined every tiny event, is replaced with what the Bible shows of how God dealt with Adam, Cain, Jonah, Paul and Peter (to name a few), all these problems disappear.

1. *God is no longer the cause of evil,*
2. *People are punished for what they themselves decided to do.*
3. *Love is a reality* as people can decide to obey God and love Him or not.
4. *Prayer becomes the act of joining God in what He is doing,* bringing a real difference into the world.

5. *Evangelism is necessary,* for faith comes by hearing, not automatically from being chosen without reference to belief.

Conclusion

God is sovereign. In His sovereignty, He has created mankind in His image.

As part of this He has given human beings a degree of ability to choose. He has made us agents who can be the "first cause" of events, just as He Himself is a "first cause."

God commands and expects us to obey, but does not prevent us from choosing otherwise, within limits that He has set. This is seen every day in the disobedience of believers and the obedience of unbelievers.

Scripturally there is no sound evidence that God foreordains every act of every person for all of history. There are passages that can be interpreted that way, but looking at the context, especially the overarching context of the whole Bible quickly shows the fallacy of such a view.

Conclusion thus far? I cannot be a Calvinist if it means accepting the Calvinistic view of God's sovereignty.

Chapter 15
A Look at the Calvinist TULIP

The concise description of Calvinism is found in their acronym TULIP. At one time, after hearing a brief definition of each point, I thought I was a four point Calvinist. But after looking at each petal more in depth, I realized I could not be a Calvinist on any one of the points. Here is what I found.

Point 1: <u>T</u>ULIP: Total Depravity

T stands for Total Depravity. The Westminster Confession of Faith states. "Our first parents...became dead in sin, and wholly defiled in all the faculties and parts of soul and body...wholly inclined to all evil. ... Man, by his fall into a state of sin, hath wholly lost all ability of will to any spiritual good accompanying salvation ... being altogether adverse from that good and dead to sin, is not able by his own strength, to convert himself or to prepare himself there unto."[28]

At first glance this seems to fit the biblical picture of mankind after the fall: blind, alienated, uninterested, rebellious.

- "And even if our gospel is veiled, it is veiled to those who are perishing. The god of this age has blinded the minds of unbelievers, so that they cannot see the light of the gospel of the glory of Christ, who is the image of God." (2Co. 4:3,4)

- "There is no one who understands, no one who seeks God...there is no one who does good, not even one." (Romans 3:11,12b).

- "...the sinful mind is hostile to God. It does not submit to God's law, nor can it do so" (Rom. 8:7).

However, this is only one part of the biblical picture. No mention is made of the ongoing work of God which makes it possible for fallen mankind to respond to the work of Christ and

---

[28] *Westminster Confession of Faith* (London: n.p. 1643), VI:ii,iv;IX:iii.

to accept the proffered forgiveness bought at the cross. The following verses outline what God is doing to make it possible for mankind to respond to the gospel.

- "The wrath of God *is being revealed* from heaven against all the ungodlessness...of men...since what may be known about God is plain to them, because God *has made it plain to them.* For since the creation of the world God's invisible qualities--his eternal power and divine nature--*have been clearly seen, being understood* from what has been made, *so that men are without excuse*" (Rom. 1:18-21; emphasis mine).

- "...the Counselor...*will convict the world* of guilt in regard to sin and righteousness and judgment..." (Jn. 16:7,8; emphasis mine).

- "John...came as *a witness to testify* concerning that light, so that through him *all men might believe"* (Jn. 1:7; emphasis mine).

- "The true light that *gives light to every man* was coming into the world" (Jn. 1:9; emphasis mine).

- "...God who said, 'Let light shine out of darkness,' *made his light shine in our hearts to give us the light of the knowledge of the glory of God in the face of Christ"* (2Co. 4:6; emphasis mine).

- "For the grace of God that brings salvation *has appeared to all men. "* (Tit. 2:11; emphasis mine)

- "God *commands all men everywhere* to repent." (Ac. 17:30; emphasis mine)

Not only is this vital aspect of the major theme of the Bible absent from this Calvinistic doctrine, but Calvinism goes even further than the biblical record with the "dead in sins" concept, comparing it to the condition of a corpse. Palmer writes: "The biblical picture, however is of a man at the bottom of the ocean...dead. If he is to be saved, then a miracle must occur. He must be brought back to life and to the surface, and then ask the guard to rescue him...."[29]

Although Arthur Pink was an extreme Calvinist, he recognized the fallacy of the corpse analogy: "A corpse in the cemetery is not a suitable analogy of the natural man. A corpse in the cemetery is incapable of performing evil! A corpse cannot 'despise and reject' Christ (Isaiah 53:3), cannot 'resist the Holy Spirit' (Acts 7:51), cannot disobey the gospel (2 Thes. 1:8); but the natural man can and does these things!"[30]

Apart from the logical fallacy, if we look at several interactions between God and fallen man, the error of this analogy immediately becomes apparent.

- After Adam had sinned, God came and talked with him and Eve; they were able to respond, to interact, and sin further. They were not "dead" like a corpse.

    As I understand it, the biblical concept of death is not end of ability to interact, but it is the concept of separation. When Adam and Eve sinned, they died spiritually, being alienated from God; they died socially, being alienated from each other; they died personally, being alienated from themselves. Then in the end they died physically, being separated from their bodies. The body is not the real person; the soul and spirit continue on.

- When Cain's sacrifice was rejected, God came and talked with him, encouraging him to do what was right; the fact that God called him to obedience infers that he was able to respond to this call. Again, after Cain murdered Able, God came and talked with him. In both cases Cain was not a dead corpse unable to interact.

- When Jesus spoke with the rich young man, they were able to interact, and the man understood clearly what

---

[29] Edwin H. Palmer, *The Five Points of Cavinism* (Baker Books, enlarged ed. 20th printing, 1999).

[30] Arthur W. Pink, *Studies in the Scriptures* (n.p. 1927), 250-261.

108

Christ asked of him, but rejected it. And Christ loved him.

Unregenerate man is not a corpse unable to interact with God; he is able to choose right and wrong within certain limits, (Jesus said that evil men can do good to their children), and with the help of God listed in the verses quoted above, is able to hear and reject or accept the gospel.

As a consequence of this false analogy, Calvinism insists that a person must first be regenerated or born again before he can have faith: "...once he is born again, he can for the first time turn to Jesus... asking Jesus to save him."[31]

R.C. Sproul states it this way: "A cardinal point of Reformed theology is the maxim, 'Regeneration precedes faith.'"[32]

John Piper says that man must first "...be born of God. Then, with the new nature of God, he immediately receives Christ." [33]

This is, of course, the opposite of the biblical pattern. Romans 10 makes this clear. "...faith comes from hearing the message and the message is heard through the word of Christ." (Rom. 10:17). "...the word of faith we are proclaiming: that if you confess with your mouth, 'Jesus is Lord' and believe in your heart that God raised him from the dead, you will be saved." (Rom. 10:8,9)

First comes the message of the gospel; then hearing, then calling to God and believing, then being saved (Rom. 10:13-15).

1 Peter makes this order very clear: "For you have been born again, not of perishable seed, but of imperishable, through the living and enduring word of God....And this is the word that was preached to you." (1Pe. 1:22,25) The Word was preached, then, as Romans says, they believed, then they were born again.

---

[31] Edwin H. Palmer, *The Five Points of Cavinism* (Baker Books, enlarged ed. 20th printing, 1999), 19.

[32] R.C. Sproul, *Chosen by God* (Tyndale House Publishers, Inc., 1986), 10.

[33] John Piper and Pastoral Staff, *Tulip: What We Believe About the Five Points of Calvinism: Position Paper of the Pastoral Staff* (Desiring God Ministry, 1997), 12.

(10:17) Galatians 3;26 echoes this: "You are all sons of God through faith in Christ Jesus...." not through first being born again.

Spurgeon, a sometime Calvinist, clearly recognized the error of the Calvinist position: "If I am to preach faith in Christ to a man who is regenerated, then the man, being regenerated is saved already, and it is an unnecessary and ridiculous thing for me to preach Christ to him, and bid him to believe in order to be saved when he is saved already, being regenerate."[34]

This Calvinist point is clearly unbiblical. One Calvinist says, "Deny this doctrine and the whole of Calvinism is demolished."[35] There you have it, but we will press on to the other points.

Point 2: T**U**LIP: Unconditional Election

U stands for Unconditional Election. The Canons of Dort declare: "That some receive the gift of faith from God and others do not receive it proceeds from God's eternal decree..[by] which decree, he graciously softens the hearts of the elect, however obstinate, and inclines them to believe, while he leaves the non-elect in his just judgment to their own wickedness and obduracy."[36]

God decides on no basis whatsoever but by the mystery of His will to save some, called the elect, and to allow all others to go to Hell even though He could save them all if He so desired.

This doctrine states that God, in the mystery of His will, unconditionally decreed that certain human beings would be elected to salvation, while the rest, also unconditionally, would be condemned to hell. Those so condemned would have no chance to believe.

Calvin himself realized that this doctrine was against reason and conscience: "The decree, I admit, is dreadful; and yet it is

---

[34] C.H. Spurgeon, "The Warrant of Faith" (Pilgrim Publications, 1978), 3. One-sermon booklet from 63-volume set.

[35] David J. Engelsma, "The Death of Confessional Calvinsim in Scottish Presbyterianism", Standard Bearer, December 1, 1992, 103.

[36] Canons of Dort (Dortrecht, Holland, 1619), 1:6.

impossible to deny that God foreknew what the end of man was to be before he made him, and foreknew, because he had so ordained by his decree."[37] Here again is the false idea that for God to foreknow He had to foreordain, which is non-biblical and illogical and an denigration to the infiniteness of His character.

The best argument against this doctrine is the Word itself.

1. *The God of the Bible is one wants all to be saved:*

- "He is patient with you, not wanting anyone to perish, but *everyone* to come to repentance" (2Pe. 3:9; emphasis mine).

- "...God our Savior who wants *all men* to be saved and come to a knowledge of the truth" (1Ti. 2:3,4; emphasis mine).

- "For the grace of God that brings salvation has appeared to *all men*." (Tit. 2:11; emphasis mine).

- "...Christ Jesus came into the world to save *sinners*–of whom I am the worst" (1Ti. 1:15; emphasis mine).

- "But I, when I am lifted up will draw *all men* to myself" (Jn. 12:32; emphasis mine).

- "...*Whoever* is thirsty, let him come; and *whoever* wishes, let him take the free gift of the water of life" (Rev. 22:17; emphasis mine).

2. *He calls all to come.*

- "God commands *all men* everywhere to repent" (Ac. 17:30; emphasis mine).

- "For God so loved the world that he gave his one and only Son, that *whoever* believes..." (Jn. 3:16; emphasis mine).

---

[37] Calvin, op. cit., III: xxiii, 7.

- "*Whoever* believes in him is not condemned..."
  (Jn 3:18; emphasis mine).

- "Rend your heart, and not your garments. *Return to the Lord your God,* for he is gracious and compassionate, slow to anger and abounding in love and he relents from sending calamity" (Joe. 2:13; emphasis mine).

- "...you are a *gracious and compassionate God,* slow to anger and abounding in love, a God who relents from sending calamity." (Jnh. 4:2; emphasis mine).

  Note that these last two verses concern first unbelieving Israelites and then the pagan, wicked gentile enemies of Israel--God has compassion on all!

  Calvinists like to use Matthew 11:27 to show how God limits who can come to Christ: "...No one knows the Son except the Father, and no one knows the Father except the Son and those to whom the Son chooses to reveal him." It is a restrictive statement, but the next verse shows to whom the Son want to reveal the Father: "Come to me, *all you* who are weary and burdened...."

3. *God Himself puts a condition on salvation, that of faith or believing,* so it is conditional.

   - "...that *whoever believes* in him shall not perish but have eternal life" (Jn. 3:16; emphasis mine).

   - "...*whoever does not believe* stands condemned already because he has not believed in the name of God's one and only son" (Jn. 3:18; emphasis mine).

   - "*Whoever believes* in the Son has eternal life..." (Jn. 3:35; emphasis mine).

   - "For we also have had the gospel preached to us, just as they [the Israelites] did; but the message they heard was of no value to them because those who heard did not combine it with faith. Now *we who have believed enter that rest...*" (Heb. 4:2,3; emphasis mine).

4. *This view violates the picture of love God Himself presents.*

- "The Lord is gracious and compassionate, slow to anger and rich in love" (Ps. 145:8).

- "The Lord is good to all; he has compassion on all he has made" (Ps. 145:9).

- "The Lord is faithful to all his promises and loving toward all he has made" (Ps. 145:13b).

- "The Lord is righteous in all his ways and loving toward all he has made" (Ps. 145:17).

- "Whoever does not love does not know God, for God is love" (1Jn. 4:8).

- "But I tell you: Love your enemies and pray for those who persecute you, that you may be sons of your Father in heaven. He causes his sun to rise on the evil and the good, and sends rain on the righteous and unrighteous." (Mt. 5:44-46)
  The example of for us to follow in loving our enemies is God's!

- "For God so loved the world that he gave his one and only Son...." (Jn. 3:16)

D.A. Carson, a Calvinist, sees the contradiction in the thought that God would condemn people to Hell without a chance to believe.

...the entire prophecy of Hosea is an astonishing portrayal of the love of God. Almighty God is likened to a betrayed and cuckolded husband. But the intensity of God's passion for the covenant nation comes to a climax in Hosea 11, "When Israel was a child," God declares "I loved him and out of Egypt I called my son. (Amos 11:1)...." But the more God loved Israel, the more they drifted away. God was the

one who cared for them...the one who "led them with cords of love and human kindness" (11:4). Yet they...sacrificed to Baals and loved idolatry. So God promises judgment. They will return to "Egypt" and Assyria, i.e., to captivity and slavery, "because they refuse to repent" (11:5). Their cities will be destroyed (11:6). ... Thus it sounds as if implacable judgment has been pronounced. But then it is almost as if God cannot endure the thought. In an agony of emotional intensity, God cries,

"How can I give you up, Ephraim? How can I hand you over, Israel? My heart is changed within me; all my compassion is aroused. I will not carry out my fierce anger.... For I am God and not man... I will not come in wrath..... I will settle them in their homes." declares the Lord."[38]

God is passionate in His desire to see all come to Him, and as we know, not all the Israelites turned to God, yet He pursued them. He loves, yearns for and calls to not just the elect, but all men.

Calvin taught that God loves only the elect (in all his Institutes, he does not mention once God's love for the non-elect), but Scripture clearly teaches otherwise. The God of the Bible loves all his creation, all people, good and bad. He will punish the wicked (those who refuse the truth), but according to Scripture He loves them none-the-less: "For God so loved the world..." (Jn. 3:16). In contrast, the God of the Calvinist loves only the elect; the rest He gives zero opportunity to love Him, to come to know Him, to spend eternity in heaven. Why? It is the mystery of God's will, the Calvinist says. This, however, does not line up with the God we have been looking at in Scripture.

Even Calvinist R.C. Sproul, honestly looking at this extra-biblical belief, has to say, "If some people are not elected unto salvation, then it would seem that God is not at all loving toward them. Further, it seems that it would have been more

---

[38] D.A. Carson, *The Difficult Doctrine of God's Love* (Crossway Books, 2000), 46-47.

loving of God not to have allowed to be born. That may indeed be the case."[39]

Calvinists somehow feel that if men can choose to accept Christ without being unconditionally chosen to do so, it is both a slap at God's sovereignty and is an attempt to earn salvation, a work. "By making election conditional upon something that man does, even if what he does is simply to repent and believe the gospel, God's grace is seriously compromised."[40] Another Calvinist says, "To reject [Calvinistic] election is to reject salvation by grace and promote salvation by works."[41]

However, Scripture teaches otherwise: "By grace you are saved through faith...not of works...."(Eph 2:8,9). This Calvinistic view is not only false Scripturally, it is a false either/or statement. God's grace is dependent on God's character, not on what we do! And Calvinists then contradict their position by saying that if one of the elect believes after being "regenerated" then it is not a work.

This point really is the crux of Calvinistic doctrine: if a human being can believe in response to the gospel with the working of the Holy Spirit (as pointed out by all the verses in the section on Total Depravity), then Calvinism is absolutely wrong. And this is the case. Salvation is conditional, on believing, not on election.

Point 3: TU<u>L</u>IP: Limited Atonement

L stands for Limited Atonement. Dort declares: "For this was the sovereign counsel, and most gracious will and purpose of God the Father, that...the most precious death of his Son should extend to all the elect...all those, and those only, who were from eternity chosen to salvation...he purchased...by his death."[42]

These elect are the only ones for whom Christ died in payment for the penalty for their sins and that His death is efficacious for no others.

---

[39] R.C. Sproul, *Chosen by God* (Tyndale House Publishers, Inc., 1986), 32.

[40] C. Samuel Storms, *Chosen for Life* (Baker Book House, 1987), 55.

[41] Carl Morton, *The Berean Baptist Banner,* January 5, 1995, 19.

[42] Canons of Dort (Dortrecht, Holland, 1619), II:8.

Comparing this idea (that Christ's sacrifice was only for the elect and not for all the other people in the world) with Scripture and with Calvin's own commentaries on such verses (see pages 119-121) easily brings one to a proper solution.

Look at these verses:

"He is the atoning sacrifice *for our sins,* and not only for ours, but *also for the sins of the whole world*" (1 Jn. 2:2; emphasis mine). Here John is writing to believers, talking about "our sins", that is the sins of the elect. The he speaks of the other category, the unbelievers, "the sins of the whole world." Jesus, says the Apostle John, died for both.

However, what Calvinists want us to believe is that this word "world" (*kosmos*) refers not to everyone, but only to the elect. That is, in order to maintain this doctrine of limited atonement, they must redefine Greek words in the New Testament. Therefore, "world" "all" "everyone" become "the elect" "all the elect" "everyone who is elect."

In the example above of 1 John 2:2, this clearly cannot be the case because John distinguishes between the sins of believers and those of the world. Then he goes on in verse 15 to clarify what he means when he uses the word "world" (*kosmos*).

"*Do not love the world or anything in the world. If anyone loves the world, the love of the Father is not in him.*" (1 Jn. 2:15) If John were referring to the elect, this would be a strange command, not to love (the elect). "World" here can only mean the world system including all unbelievers. John is consistent in his use of "world" throughout his writings.

Having said that, it is important to point out that there are instances in Scripture where "world" does not mean all the people in the world, but it is obvious from the context from the intent (it is a geographical reference) and who is speaking (those who opposed Christ). For instance, in John 12:19, Jesus' enemies expressed frustration and used local exaggeration to express this. "So the Pharisees said to one another, 'See, this is getting us nowhere. Look how the whole world has gone after him'" (Mt. 18:7).

These exceptions, however do not negate the normal use of world in John's and other writers' passages. We will be looking at other verses dealing with who Christ died for, but before that, let's look at some other uses of the word "world." See what you think is the definition of "world" in these.

- "Woe to the world because of things that cause people to sin! Such things must come, but woe to the man through whom they come." (Mt. 18:7)

- "The true light that gives light to every man was coming into the world" (Jn 1:9).

- "He was in the world and though the world was made through him the world did not recognize him" (Jn. 1:10).

- "For the bread of God is he who comes down from heaven and gives life to the world" (Jn. 6:33)

- "I am not praying for the world, but for those you have given me for they are yours" (Jn. 17:9).

These are not about whom Jesus died for, but obviously are speaking about the whole cosmic system, including to whole sum of people.

One Calvinist told me that unless every use of "world" (*kosmos*) in the NT meant "all the people in the world" then none could mean that. In fact, the opposite is true, all we need is one instance of "world" (*kosmos*) meaning all people for Jesus' death to be for everyone. And 1 John 2:2 clearly provides that. However, there are dozens of other passages which say the same thing. Here is a sampling of them:

- "For there is one God and on mediator between God and men, the man Christ Jesus, who gave himself as a *ransom for all men."* (1Ti. 2:5,6; emphasis mine).

- "...the living God, who is the *Savior of all men,* and *especially of those who believe*" (1Ti. 4:10; emphasis mine). Note the distinction between those all men and those who believe, clearly stating that Christ's death is for the sins of the whole world.

- "...the Father has sent his Son to be the *Savior of the world*" (1Jn. 4:14).

- "Look, the Lamb of God who takes away *the sin of the world!*" (Jn. 1:29; emphasis mine)

- "....we know that this man really is *the Savior of the world*" (Jn. 4:42; emphasis mine).

- "And if any man hear my words, and believe not, I judge him not: for I came not to judge the world, but *to save the world*" (Jn. 12:47; emphasis mine).

- "...Jesus Christ the righteous One. He is the atoning *sacrifice for our sins, and not only for ours but also for the sins of the whole world.*" (1Jn 2:2)

- "But we see Jesus...now crowned with glory and honor because he suffered death, so that by the grace of God he might *taste death for everyone*" (Heb. 2:9; emphasis mine).

- "Consequently, just as the result of one trespass was *condemnation for all men,* so also the result of one act of righteousness was justification that brings *life for all men*" (Rom. 5:18; emphasis mine).

I think that gives enough of a sampling to get the point across, but we will not end here. There is a surprise addition to this argument against limited atonement. Here are John Calvin's own thoughts on some of these verses we have looked at. Draw your own conclusions on where he stood on limited atonement.

1. "Look, the Lamb of God who takes away the sin of the world!" (Jn. 1:29)
   Calvin writes, "And when he says 'the sin of the whole world' he extends this kindness indiscriminately to *the whole human race,* that the Jews might not think the Redeemer has been sent to them alone. From this we infer that *the whole world* is bound in the same condemnation; and that since all men without exception are guilty of unrighteousness before God, they have need of reconciliation. John, therefore, by speaking of the *sin of the world in general,* wanted to make us feel our own misery and exhort us to seek the remedy. Now it is for us to embrace the *blessing offered to all,* that

each may make up his mind that there is nothing to hinder him from finding reconciliation in Christ if only, led by faith, he comes to him."[43]

2. "....we know that this man really is the Savior of the world" (Jn. 4:42).

Calvin writes, "Again, when they proclaim that Jesus is the Savior of the world and the Christ, they have undoubtedly learned this from hearing Him. From this we infer that in two days Christ taught the sum of the Gospel more plainly there than He had so far done in Jerusalem. And He declared that the salvation He had brought was *common to the whole world,* so that they should understand more easily that it belonged to them also."[44]

3. "And if any man hear my words, and believe not, I judge him not: for I came not to judge the world, but to save the world" (Jn. 12:47).

Calvin writes: "For He delayed pronouncing judgement on them because He had come rather *for the salvation of all*...Because He had temporarily laid aside the office of judge and *offers salvation to all* indiscriminately and stretches out His arms *to embrace all, that all may* be the more encouraged to repent. And yet He heightens by an important detail the crime of rejecting an invitation so kind and gracious; for it is as if He had said: 'See, *I have come to call all*; and forgetting the role of judge, my one aim is to attract and rescue from destruction those who already seem doubly ruined.' Hence *no man is condemned for despising the Gospel save he who spurns the lovely news of salvation and deliberately decides to bring destruction on himself.*" (Note how this contradicts unconditional election)[45]

---

[43] Calvin's Commentary on John 1:28,29; emphasis mine.

[44] Calvin's Commentary on John 4:42; emphasis mine.

[45] Calvin's Commentary on John 12:47; emphasis mine

4. "I am the way, the truth and the life. No man comes unto the father but by me." (Jn. 14:6)

   Calvin writes: "Christ's proper work was to appease the wrath of God by atoning for *the sins of the world*, to redeem men from death and to procure righteousness and life."[46]

5. "...for the prince of this world cometh, and hath nothing in me" (Jn. 14:30).

   Calvin writes: "For in *the word 'world' is here embraced the whole human race*....For it was God who appointed his Son to be the Reconciler and determined that *the sins of the world* should be expiated by His death."[47]

6. "And when he is come, he will reprove the world of sin, and of righteousness and of judgment..." (Jn. 16:8).

   Calvin writes: "I think that *under the word 'world' are included both those who were to be truly converted to Christ and hypocrites and reprobates.*"[48]

7. "Consequently, just as the result of one trespass was condemnation for all men, so also the result of one act of righteousness was justification that brings life for all men" (Rom. 5:18).

   Calvin writes: "*Paul makes grace common to all men*, not because it in fact extends to all, but because *it is offered to all*. Although *Christ suffered for the sins of the world*, and is offered by the goodness of God without distinction *to all men*, yet not all receive Him."[49]

8. "He bore the sins of many" (Isa. 53:12).

   Calvin writes, "I approve of the ordinary reading, that He alone bore the punishment of many, because *on Him was laid the guilt of the whole world.* It is evident

---

[46] Calvin's Commentary on John 14:6; emphasis mine.

[47] Calvin's Commentary on John 14:30; emphasis mine.

[48] Calvin's Commentary on John 16:8; emphasis mine.

[49] Calvin's Commentary on Romans 5:18; emphasis mine.

from other passages, and especially from the fifth chapter of the Epistle to the Romans, that *'many'* *sometimes denotes 'all.'*"[50]

9. "So Christ was once offered to bear the sins of many" (Heb. 9:28).

    Calvin writes,"To 'bear the sins of many' means to free those who have sinned from their guilt by His satisfaction. He says *many meaning all,* as in Romans 5:15. It is of course certain that not all enjoy the fruits of Christ's death, but this happens because *their unbelief hinders them.*"[51] Not their not being the elect.

10. "In whom we have redemption through his blood even the forgiveness of sins" (Col. 1:14).

    Calvin writes: "He says that this redemption was procured 'by the blood of Christ,' for by the sacrifice of His death *all the sins of the world have been expiated.*"[52]

Limited atonement is clearly neither Scriptural nor according to Calvin's own commentaries. Please understand that no claim is being made to Calvin's consistency on this, but it is noteworthy that when operating outside of his "Institutes" and looking at Scripture itself, Calvin came to biblical conclusions.

Point 4: TUL**I**P: Irresistible Grace

"I" stands for Irresistible Grace. The Westminster confession states: "All those whom God hath predestinated unto life, and those only, he is pleased, in his appointed and accepted time, effectually to call, by his word and Spirit, out of that state of sin and death...effectually drawing them to Jesus Christ; yet so, as they come most freely, being made willing by his grace."[53]

---

[50] Calvin's Commentary on Isaiah 53:12; emphasis mine.

[51] Calvin's Commentary on Hebrews 9:28; emphasis mine.

[52] Calvin's Commentary on Colossians 1:14; emphasis mine.

[53] Westminster, op. cit., X:I.

God is able to cause whomever He will to respond to the gospel, that without this enabling no one could do so, and that He only provides this Irresistible Grace to the elect and damns the rest.

Piper says, "...new birth is the effect of irresistible grace...an act of sovereign creation...."[54]

That is, the elect will come to God whether they want to or not. God overcomes their will with his irresistible grace. This point flows from the previous ones: since man is unable to respond to the gospel (total depravity), God must unconditionally choose him (unconditional election), prepare the way by limited atonement, and then force him to come via irresistible grace. Without the earlier points, it would not make sense. And it does not make biblical sense, especially as we consider all the biblical data presented above.

One Calvinist writer attempts to use Scripture to explain it this way, "...the Gospel of Christ is the power of God unto salvation! Nothing can stop it. ... If God's grace can be successfully resisted, then God can be overcome...."[55] p291

Dave Hunt answers thusly, "God's power in salvation refers to His ability to pay the penalty so that He can be just and yet justify sinners; it does not refer to His forcing salvation upon those who would otherwise reject it.... Always it is 'whosoever will come', never the imposition of God's grace upon any unwilling person."[56]

So, the Calvinist believes that it is God's irresistible grace that brings people to salvation, the elect that is.

Three other points must be added here.

First, Calvinists believe that irresistible grace must first bring regeneration to a person, the new birth, before he can believe. Here are some quotes by Calvinists on this subject.

---

[54] John Piper and Pastoral Staff, *Tulip: What We Believe About the Five Points of Calvinism: Position Paper of the Pastoral Staff* (Desiring God Ministry, 1997), 12.

[55] C.D. Cole, *Definitions of Doctrines* (Bible Truth Depot n.d.), 84.

[56] Dave Hunt, *What Love is This?: Calvinism's Misrepresentation of God* (Loyal Publishing, 2002, Sisters, Oregon), p 286.

A person is regenerated before he believes.[57]

A man is not saved because he believes in Christ, but he believes in Christ because he has been regenerated.[58]

We do not believe in order to be born again; we are born again in order that we may believe. [59]

White, reacting to Geisler's book, *Chosen But Free*, writes in support of the Calvinistic view, "...if a person can have saving faith without the new birth, then *what does the new birth accomplish*? Evidently one does not need the new birth to obey God's commands or have saving faith."[60]

All Mr. White has to do is read Acts 16:31 to understand: "Believe on the Lord Jesus Christ, and you shall be saved." First faith, then the new birth. Hebrews 4:2 reiterates this truth: "...the message they [the Israelites] heard was of no value to them, because those who heard did not combine it with faith" (Heb.4:2).

Scripture consistently makes faith the basis for salvation, not regeneration beforehand. Here are a few verses that point this out:

"...*to those who believed on his name* he gave the right to become children of God" (Jn. 1:12; emphasis mine).

"...whoever *believes in him* shall not perish but have eternal life" (Jn. 3:16b; emphasis mine).

"*Believe on the Lord Jesus Christ*, and you shall be saved" (Ac. 16:31; emphasis mine).

"For in the gospel a righteousness from God is revealed, a righteousness that is by faith from first to last, just as it is written, '*The righteous will live by faith*'" (Rom. 1:17; emphasis mine).

---

[57] W.E. Best, *Simple Faith (A Misnomer)* (W.E.Best Book Missionary Trust, 1993), 34.

[58] Boettner, op. cit., 101.

[59] Grover E. Gunn, *The Doctrines of Grace* (Footstool Publications, 1987), 8.

[60] James R. White, *The Potters Freedom* (Calvary Press Publishing, 2000), 185.

"...to the man who does not work but trusts God who justifies the wicked, *his faith is credited as righteousness.*" (Rom. 4:5; emphasis mine).

"For by grace are ye saved *through faith...*" (Eph. 2:8; emphasis mine). There is no mention of regeneration first.

Second, Calvinists believe that after the irresistible grace of God has regenerated one of the elect, then he is given faith as a gift so he can believe. Mathison writes: "Saving faith is the gift of God, a result of the regenerating work of the Holy Spirit."[61]

Clark explains it more clearly, "A dead man cannot...exercise faith in Jesus Christ. Faith is an activity of spiritual life, and without the life there can be no activity. Furthermore, faith...does not come by any independent decision. Scripture is explicit, plain and unmistakable: 'For by grace are ye saved through faith, and that not of yourselves, it is the gift of God' (Ephesians 2:8) Look at the words again, 'It is the gift of God.' If God does not give a man faith, no amount of will power and decision can manufacture it for him."[62]

Looking at the English of Ephesians 2:8 is enough to see that the "it" of the gift refers not to faith, but to the salvation offered. Looking at the Greek confirms this. Greek scholar F. F. Bruce, himself a Calvinist, puts it this way: "The fact that the demonstrative pronoun 'that' is neuter in Greek (*tauto*), whereas 'faith' is a feminine noun (*pistis*), combines with other considerations to suggest that it is the whole concept of salvation by grace through faith that is described as the gift of God. This incidentally, was Calvin's interpretation."[63]

What Calvin said on the subject was, "But they commonly misinterpret this text, and restrict the word 'gift' to faith alone. But Paul ... does not mean that faith is the gift of God, but that salvation is given to us by God...."[64] Note that this quote is from

[61] Keith A. Mathison, *Dispensationalism: Rightly Dividing the People of God?* (Presbyterian and Reformed Publishing Company, 1995), 99.

[62] Gordon H. Clark, *Predestination* (Presbyterian and Reformed Publishing Company, 1987), 102.

[63] F.F. Bruce, *The Epistles to the Colossians, Philemon and the Ephesians* (Wm. B. Eerdmans Pub. Co., 1984), 220-221.

[64] John Calvin, *Calvin's New Testament Commentaries* (Wm. B. Eerdmans' Pub. Co., 1994), 11:145.

his commentaries where he is dealing with Scripture rather than his *Institutes* where he dealt more with Augustine.

Contrary to the Calvinist idea, Scripture declares that eternal life is the gift: "...the gift of God is eternal life in Jesus Christ our Lord" (Rom. 6:23).

Faith comes from hearing the Word: "...faith comes from hearing the message, and the message is heard through the word of Christ." (Rom. 10:17).

Third, this doctrine produces a very serious dilemma for those who believe it. If God can, with irresistible grace, bring unwilling elect sinners to the new birth, to salvation, is there any reason why He could not do this with the rest of the sinners? The answer is obviously, "No!"

The Calvinist says that God elected some for Haven and the rest for Hell because of the mystery of His will. Those elected can be forced (made willing with irresistible grace) to have faith and believe. If God could do that for everyone but chooses not to, what can we conclude? What does this say about His love, His justice, His many stated invitations to all? The contradiction with Scripture and the character of God is obvious.

Think of this as an example. Suppose you come across an accident with 4 people unconscious in a car that has run into a tree and has just caught on fire. The two in the back are obviously Hindus from their garb, while the two in the front appear to be Christians by the Bibles they have next to them. You decide to rescue only the Christians, leaving the Hindus to their fate, although you could have easily rescued them, too.

How does that fit in with God's command to love our neighbors as ourselves, to love our enemies, to do good to all, as He does? It doesn't! And if our decision and actions were known to the authorities, we could be charged with at least manslaughter.

Such an action of selective salvation does not fit with God's character either. If irresistible grace were a reality, God would be open to the same legitimate charge of not being loving: He could forcibly save all people, but chooses not to, because it brings Him glory to not save some! That is certainly contrary to His character as presented in Scripture.

The biblical position of God preparing salvation for all, working to bring them to a place of understanding, calling them to believe and be saved, avoids this terrible description of God. It is the choice of men to believe or not, not God's arbitrary condemnation of billions to hell.

"Whoever believes in him is not condemned, but whoever does not believe stands condemned already *because they have not believed* in the name of God's one and only Son" (Jn. 3:18; emphasis mine).

Irresistible grace does not line up with Scripture nor with reason.

Point 5: TUL**IP**: Perseverance of the Saints

"P" stands for Perseverance of the saints: that God will not allow any of the elect to lose salvation which He has sovereignly given them.

The Westminster Confession states: "They, whom God hath accepted in his Beloved, effectually called, and sanctified by His Spirit, can neither totally nor finally fall away from the state of grace, but shall certainly preserve therein to the end, and be eternally saved. This perseverance of the saints depends not upon their own free will, but upon the immutability of the decree of the election."[65]

On the surface, one could agree with this, as it is biblical to believe in the permanency of salvation. The problem with this position is two-fold. First, this doctrine promotes the idea that one can *only* know he is of the elect by virtue of his perseverance in following Christ. How does one know when he has done enough as a Christian to have persevered?

One author said, "The result of this theology is disastrous. Since, according to Puritan belief, the genuiness of a man's faith can only be determined by the life that follows it, assurance of salvation becomes impossible at the moment of conversion."[66]

---

[65] Westminster, op. cit., XVII:i,ii.

[66] Zane C. Hodges, *The Gospel Under Seige* (Kerugma Inc., 2nd edition, 1992), vi.

Piper writes, "We must own up to the fact that our final salvation is made contingent upon the subsequent obedience which comes from faith."[67]

The result? No one can know for sure he's saved because no one lives a perfect life; did I do enough to prove my being one of the elect? R.T. Kendal wrote, "Nearly all the Puritan 'divines' when through great doubt and despair on their deathbeds as they realized their lives did not give perfect evidence that they were the elect."[68]

This doctrine of perseverance contradicts specific biblical statements saying we can know if we are saved, as the ones following illustrate.

"This is the testimony: God has given us eternal life, and this life is in his Son. *He who has the Son has life*; he who does not have the Son of God does not have life. I write these things to you who believe in the name of the Son of God *so that you may know that you have eternal life*" (1Jn. 5:11-13; emphasis mine).

Jesus said, "I tell you the truth, whoever hears my word and believes him who sent me *has eternal life and will not be condemned;* he *has crossed over* from death to life" (Jn. 5:24; emphasis mine).

"*Whoever believes in the Son has eternal life,* but whoever rejects the Son will not see life, for God's wrath remains on him" (Jn. 3:36; emphasis mine).

These assurances of salvation do not, of course, give license to sin; we are called to a holy life because God is holy. The statement of God is that, if we believe, we are saved; if we are saved our sanctification will follow, but we will all sin along the way, as did Paul, Peter, Luther and Billy Graham, but hopefully not willfully.

Second, if our perseverance were the source of our assurance of salvation, there would always be a question mark in our minds. How much perseverance is enough? Every one of us sins every day in motive, thought, word or deed. Most of

---

[67] John Piper and Pastoral Staff, *Tulip: What We Believe About the Five Points of Calvinism: Position Paper of the Pastoral Staff* (Desiring God Ministry, 1997), 25.

[68] R.T. Kendall, *Calvin and English Calvinism to 1649* (Oxford University Press, 1979), 2.

these are, hopefully, not planned or intentional sins, but are sins none the less.

Are our sins an indication that we are not of the elect; is there a "cut off point" where our sins prove us to be of the reprobate, or are we safe as long as they are not too gross?

Those Calvinists who have seriously considered this issue have struggled with doubts about their salvation, especially since Calvin said that God can give a false sense of being saved in order to keep the non-elect from being saved.

Third, and more seriously, this doctrine actually does what Calvinists so strongly oppose. It adds works to the salvation Jesus has provided. We must perform to ensure our eternal life. The proof of this belief is the anguish that many famous Calvinists experienced in the uncertainty of whether their obedience was enough to give assurance of salvation. And Piper admits it in his comment cited above: , "We must own up to the fact that our final salvation is made contingent upon the subsequent obedience which comes from faith."[69] Works salvation!

This doctrine is the opposite of what Scripture teaches— that good works flow out of our salvation, not that our good works preserve our salvation. As it says in Ephesians 2:8-10, "For it is *by grace you have been saved, through faith*—and this is not from yourselves, it is the gift of God— *not by works*, so that no one can boast. For we are God's handiwork, *created in Christ Jesus to do good works*, which God prepared in advance for us to do" (emphasis mine).

So the fifth petal of Tulip also fails the test of Scripture, also.

---

[69] John Piper and Pastoral Staff, *Tulip: What We Believe About the Five Points of Calvinism: Position Paper of the Pastoral Staff* (Desiring God Ministry, 1997), 25.

Chapter 16
Conclusion of the Issue

This personal study of Calvinism leaves me with a clear and biblical conclusion that every aspect of Tulip goes beyond Scripture because of overemphasis and extrapolation on truth. Therefore, I cannot in good conscience be a Calvinist—nor an Arminian, who also goes beyond the bounds of Scripture—but must stand in the middle of the two with both feet firmly planted in the Word.

This third option states that God is Sovereign. Man has responsibility for his decisions. God has provided all for salvation. He also enables all to accept or reject His offer. It is willful unbelief, not God's decision that send people to Hell. It is faith accepted that brings salvation. This is biblical Christianity, and here I stand.

Made in United States
Orlando, FL
29 October 2022

23977180R00072